HERSHEY'S

CHOCOLATE LOVER'S

COOKBOOK

HERSHEY'S
CHOCOLATE LOVER'S
C O O K B O O K

WILTON HOUSE

Wilton House is an imprint of Joshua Morris Publishing, Inc.

Produced by Joshua Morris Publishing, Inc., 221 Danbury Rd., Wilton, CT 06897.

All recipes developed and tested in the Hershey Kitchens. Designed by Sandi Kroll.
Photography on pages iii, 1, 4, 8 15-19, 24, 34, 35, 39, 43-46, 53-58, 60-63, 67-69, 72-75, 79-81, 85, 89, 91, 93, 103-107, 111-115, 119, 124, 128-131, 134, 136-149, 152, 154-157, 160, 163, 164, 169, 172, 173 and 176-183 by Stephany Molenko.
Food styling for these photographs by Elizabeth Thomas Hanna.
Prop styling for these photographs and photographs on pages 3, 5, 6, 20, 25, 32 and 110, by Richard H. Bach.

10 9 8 7 6 5 4

ISBN: 0-88705-761-6

TABLE OF CONTENTS

TRIPLE CHOCOLATE TORTE

2 eggs, separated
1½ cups sugar, divided
1¼ cups all-purpose flour
½ cup HERSHEY'S Cocoa
¾ teaspoon baking soda
½ teaspoon salt
½ cup vegetable oil
1 cup buttermilk or sour milk*
Chocolate Cream Filling
Chocolate Glaze
Chocolate Leaves or Chocolate
  Curls (optional, see page
  181 or 177)

Chocolate Cream Filling
⅔ cup sugar
⅓ cup HERSHEY'S Cocoa
1½ cups cold whipping cream
1½ teaspoons vanilla extract

Chocolate Glaze
3 tablespoons butter or
  margarine
3 tablespoons light corn syrup
1 tablespoon water
1 cup HERSHEY'S Semi-Sweet
  Chocolate Chips

▼ Heat oven to 350°F. Grease and flour two 9-inch round baking pans. In small mixer bowl, beat egg whites until foamy; gradually add ½ cup sugar, beating until stiff peaks form.

▼ In large mixer bowl, stir together remaining 1 cup sugar, flour, cocoa, baking soda and salt. Add oil, buttermilk and egg yolks; beat until smooth. Gently fold egg whites into batter. Pour batter into prepared pans.

▼ Bake 25 to 30 minutes or until cake springs back when touched lightly in center. Cool 5 minutes; remove from pans to wire racks. Cool completely.

▼ With long serrated knife, cut each cake layer horizontally in half. Spread one cake layer with one-third of Chocolate Cream Filling; top with second layer. Repeat procedure ending with plain layer on top.

▼ Prepare Chocolate Glaze; glaze cake. Decorate with Chocolate Leaves, if desired. Refrigerate until serving time. Cover; refrigerate leftover torte.
8 to 10 servings.

▼ CHOCOLATE CREAM FILLING: In small mixer bowl, combine sugar and cocoa. Add whipping cream and vanilla; beat on low speed of electric mixer until blended. Beat on medium speed until stiff.
About 3 cups filling.

▼ CHOCOLATE GLAZE: In small saucepan, combine butter, light corn syrup and water. Cook over medium heat, stirring constantly, until mixture begins to boil. Remove from heat; add chocolate chips, stirring until melted. Cool to room temperature.
About 1 cup glaze.

* To sour milk: Use 1 tablespoon white vinegar plus milk to equal 1 cup.

Note: 2 heart-shaped pans may be substituted for round pans.

Triple Chocolate Torte

GLAZED CRANBERRY MINI-CAKES

⅓ cup butter or margarine, softened

⅓ cup granulated sugar

⅓ cup packed light brown sugar

1 egg

1¼ teaspoons vanilla extract

1⅓ cups all-purpose flour

¾ teaspoon baking powder

¼ teaspoon baking soda

¼ teaspoon salt

2 tablespoons milk

1¼ cups coarsely chopped fresh cranberries

½ cup coarsely chopped walnuts

⅔ cup HERSHEY'S Vanilla Milk Chips

Vanilla Glaze

Vanilla Glaze

1 cup HERSHEY'S Vanilla Milk Chips

2 tablespoons vegetable oil

▼ Heat oven to 350°F. Lightly grease or paper-line small muffin cups (1¾ inches in diameter). In small mixer bowl, beat butter, granulated sugar, brown sugar, egg and vanilla extract until light and fluffy.

▼ Stir together flour, baking powder, baking soda and salt; gradually mix into butter mixture. Add milk; stir until blended. Stir in cranberries, walnuts and vanilla milk chips. Fill cups about ⅞ full with batter.

▼ Bake 18 to 20 minutes or until wooden pick inserted in center comes out clean. Cool 5 minutes; remove from pans to wire racks. Cool completely.

▼ Prepare Vanilla Glaze; drizzle over top of mini-cakes. Refrigerate 10 minutes to set glaze.
About 3 dozen mini-cakes.

▼ VANILLA GLAZE: In small microwave-safe bowl, place vanilla milk chips; sprinkle oil over chips. Microwave at HIGH (100%) 30 seconds; stir vigorously. If necessary, microwave at HIGH additional 30 seconds or just until chips are melted when stirred.

1 Grease fluted tube pans and other pans with many crevices with shortening and a pastry brush.

2 Place small amount of flour into greased pan and turn pan to coat all sides.

3 Carefully fold the fruit-nut mixture into the batter to guarantee even distribution.

Cocoa Fruitcake

¾ cup (1½ sticks) butter or
  margarine, softened
1½ cups sugar
½ teaspoon vanilla extract
¼ teaspoon brandy extract
3 eggs
1 cup all-purpose flour
6 tablespoons HERSHEY'S
  Cocoa
½ teaspoon salt
¼ teaspoon baking powder
½ cup buttermilk or sour milk*
2 cups candied red cherries,
  cut in half
1½ cups pecans, coarsely
  chopped
1 cup golden raisins
½ cup diced mixed candied fruit
Powdered sugar (optional)

▼ Heat oven to 325°F. Grease and flour 12-cup fluted tube pan. In large mixer bowl, beat butter, sugar, vanilla and brandy extract until light and fluffy. Add eggs; beat well.

▼ Stir together flour, cocoa, salt and baking powder; add alternately with buttermilk to butter mixture, beating just until blended. Stir together cherries, pecans, raisins and mixed fruit; fold into batter. Pour batter into prepared pan.

▼ Bake 1 hour and 25 minutes or until wooden pick inserted in center comes out clean. Cool 10 minutes; remove from pan. Immediately wrap in foil. Allow to stand overnight before serving. To serve, sprinkle powdered sugar over top, if desired.
12 to 16 servings.

* To sour milk: Use 1½ teaspoons white vinegar plus milk to equal ½ cup.

Glazed Cranberry Mini-Cakes, Cocoa Fruitcake

COLLECTOR'S COCOA CAKE

¾ cup (1½ sticks) butter or
  margarine, softened
1¾ cups sugar
2 eggs
1 teaspoon vanilla extract
2 cups all-purpose flour
¾ cup HERSHEY'S Cocoa or
  HERSHEY'S European Style
  Cocoa
1¼ teaspoons baking soda
½ teaspoon salt
1⅓ cups water
One-Bowl Buttercream Frosting
  or Fluffy Peanut Butter
  Frosting

▼ Heat oven to 350°F. Grease and flour two 8- or
9-inch round baking pans. In large mixer bowl, beat
butter and sugar until light and fluffy. Add eggs
and vanilla; beat on medium speed of electric mixer
1 minute.

▼ Stir together flour, cocoa, baking soda and salt; add
to butter mixture alternately with water, beating after
each addition. Pour batter into prepared pans.

▼ Bake 35 to 40 minutes for 8-inch rounds, 30 to
35 minutes for 9-inch rounds or until wooden pick
inserted in center comes out clean. Cool 10 minutes;
remove from pans to wire racks.

▼ Cool completely. Frost with One-Bowl Buttercream
Frosting or Fluffy Peanut Butter Frosting.
8 to 10 servings.
(continued)

Collector's Cocoa Cake

One-Bowl Buttercream Frosting
6 tablespoons butter or
 margarine, softened
2⅔ cups powdered sugar
½ cup HERSHEY'S Cocoa or
 HERSHEY'S European Style
 Cocoa
⅓ cup milk
1 teaspoon vanilla extract

Fluffy Peanut Butter Frosting
1 cup milk
3 tablespoons all-purpose flour
1 cup sugar
½ cup REESE'S Creamy
 Peanut Butter
½ cup shortening
1 teaspoon vanilla extract
Dash salt

▼ ONE-BOWL BUTTERCREAM FROSTING: In small mixer bowl, beat butter. Add powdered sugar and cocoa alternately with milk; beat to spreading consistency (additional milk may be needed). Blend in vanilla.
About 2 cups frosting.

▼ FLUFFY PEANUT BUTTER FROSTING: In small saucepan, gradually stir milk into flour. Cook over low heat, stirring constantly, until very thick. Transfer to small mixer bowl; press plastic wrap directly on surface. Cool to room temperature, about ½ hour. Add sugar, peanut butter, shortening, vanilla and salt. Beat on high speed of electric mixer until mixture becomes fluffy and sugar is completely dissolved.
About 3 cups frosting.

*B*LACK MAGIC CAKE

2 cups sugar
1¾ cups all-purpose flour
¾ cup HERSHEY'S Cocoa
2 teaspoons baking soda
1 teaspoon baking powder
1 teaspoon salt
2 eggs
1 cup strong black coffee or 2
 teaspoons powdered instant
 coffee plus 1 cup boiling water
1 cup buttermilk or sour milk *
½ cup vegetable oil
1 teaspoon vanilla extract

▼ Heat oven to 350°F. Grease and flour 13 x 9 x 2-inch baking pan. In large mixer bowl, stir together sugar, flour, cocoa, baking soda, baking powder and salt.

▼ Add eggs, coffee, buttermilk, oil and vanilla; beat on medium speed of electric mixer 2 minutes (batter will be thin). Pour batter into prepared pan.

▼ Bake 35 to 40 minutes or until wooden pick inserted in center comes out clean. Cool completely in pan on wire rack. Frost as desired.
12 to 15 servings.

* To sour milk: Use 1 tablespoon white vinegar plus milk to equal 1 cup.

CHOCOLATE LAYERED ANGEL CAKE

1 box (about 15 oz.) angel food
  cake mix
¼ cup HERSHEY'S Cocoa or
  HERSHEY'S European
  Style Cocoa
Chocolate Glaze

Chocolate Glaze
⅓ cup sugar
¼ cup water
1 cup HERSHEY'S Semi-Sweet
  Chocolate Chips

▼ Move oven rack to lowest position. Heat oven to 375°F. Mix cake as directed on package.

▼ Measure 4 cups batter into separate bowl; sift cocoa gradually over this batter, folding until well blended, being careful not to deflate batter. Alternately spoon plain and chocolate batters into ungreased 10-inch tube pan.

▼ Bake 30 to 35 minutes or until top crust is firm and looks very dry. Do *not* underbake. Invert pan on heat-proof funnel or bottle; cool completely, at least 1½ hours.

▼ Carefully run knife along side of pan to loosen cake; remove from pan. Place on serving plate; drizzle with Chocolate Glaze.
18 servings.

▼ CHOCOLATE GLAZE: In small saucepan, combine sugar and water. Cook over medium heat, stirring constantly, until mixture boils. Stir until sugar dissolves; remove from heat. Immediately add chocolate chips; stir until chips are melted and mixture is smooth. Cool to desired consistency; use immediately.
About ⅔ cup glaze.

1 Spoon chocolate and vanilla batters into tube pan.

2 Always cool angel cakes upside down on a funnel or bottle.

3 Before removing cake from pan, loosen cake from pan with knife drawn around inside of pan.

Chocolate Layered Angel Cake

STREUSEL APPLE-SPICE CAKE

½ cup (1 stick) butter or
  margarine, softened
1 cup sugar
2 eggs
1 teaspoon vanilla extract
2¼ cups all-purpose flour
¾ teaspoon baking powder
¾ teaspoon ground cinnamon
½ teaspoon baking soda
¼ teaspoon ground cloves
⅛ teaspoon salt
¾ cup milk
1½ cups chopped, peeled tart
  apples
¾ cup HERSHEY'S MINI
  CHIPS Semi-Sweet Chocolate
Streusel Topping
Semi-Sweet Chocolate Glaze
  (optional)

Streusel Topping
⅓ cup all-purpose flour
3 tablespoons sugar
2 tablespoons butter or
  margarine

Semi-Sweet Chocolate Glaze
3 tablespoons HERSHEY'S
  MINI CHIPS Semi-Sweet
  Chocolate
½ teaspoon shortening (do not
  use butter, margarine or oil)

▼ Heat oven to 350°F. Grease 9 x 5 x 3-inch loaf pan. In large mixer bowl, beat butter and sugar until light and fluffy. Add eggs and vanilla; beat well.

▼ Stir together flour, baking powder, cinnamon, baking soda, cloves and salt; add alternately with milk to butter mixture, blending well. Gently fold in chopped apples and small chocolate chips. Spoon batter into prepared pan.

▼ Prepare Streusel Topping; sprinkle on top of batter in pan. Bake 1 hour and 10 to 15 minutes or until wooden pick inserted in center comes out clean. Cool 10 minutes; remove from pan to wire rack.

▼ Turn right side up. Drizzle Semi-Sweet Chocolate Glaze over top, if desired. Allow glaze to set before cutting cake.
12 servings.

▼ STREUSEL TOPPING: In small bowl, stir together flour and sugar; cut in butter to form fine crumbs.

▼ SEMI-SWEET CHOCOLATE GLAZE: In small microwave-safe bowl, place small chocolate chips and shortening. Microwave at HIGH (100%) 30 to 45 seconds or until chips are melted when stirred.

CRUNCHY TOPPED COCOA CAKE

1½ **cups all-purpose flour**
1 **cup sugar**
¼ **cup HERSHEY'S Cocoa**
1 **teaspoon baking soda**
½ **teaspoon salt**
1 **cup water**
¼ **cup plus 2 tablespoons**
   vegetable oil
1 **tablespoon white vinegar**
1 **teaspoon vanilla extract**
Broiled Topping

Broiled Topping
¼ **cup (½ stick) butter or**
   margarine, softened
½ **cup packed light brown sugar**
½ **cup coarsely chopped nuts**
½ **cup flaked coconut**
3 **tablespoons light cream or**
   evaporated milk

▼ Heat oven to 350°F. Grease and flour 8-inch square baking pan. In large bowl, stir together flour, sugar, cocoa, baking soda and salt. Add water, oil, vinegar and vanilla; beat with spoon or wire whisk just until batter is smooth and ingredients are well blended. Pour batter into prepared pan.

▼ Bake 35 to 40 minutes or until wooden pick inserted in center comes out clean.

▼ Meanwhile, prepare Broiled Topping; spread on warm cake. Set oven to Broil; place cake about 4 inches from heat. Broil 3 minutes or until top is bubbly and golden brown. Remove from oven. Cool completely in pan on wire rack.
9 servings.

▼ BROILED TOPPING: In small bowl, stir together all ingredients until well blended.

Streusel Apple-Spice Cake, Crunchy Topped Cocoa Cake

PEANUTTY CHOCOLATE CHIFFON CAKE

¾ cup plus 2 tablespoons sugar, divided
¾ cup cake flour
⅓ cup HERSHEY'S Cocoa
1 teaspoon baking powder
½ teaspoon salt
¼ teaspoon baking soda
¼ cup vegetable oil
4 eggs, separated
⅓ cup cold water
1 teaspoon vanilla extract
¼ teaspoon cream of tartar
Peanut Butter Filling
Peanut Butter Glaze

Peanut Butter Filling
¾ cup miniature marshmallows
½ cup REESE'S Peanut Butter Chips
3 tablespoons milk
½ cup cold whipping cream
¼ teaspoon vanilla extract

Peanut Butter Glaze
½ cup REESE'S Peanut Butter Chips
3 tablespoons milk
1 cup powdered sugar
½ teaspoon vanilla extract

▼ Heat oven to 325°F. Very lightly spray 9-cup fluted tube pan (kugelhopf) with vegetable cooking spray.

▼ In large mixer bowl, stir together ¾ cup sugar, flour, cocoa, baking powder, salt and baking soda. Add oil, egg yolks, water and vanilla; beat until smooth.

▼ In second large mixer bowl, beat egg whites and cream of tartar until soft peaks form; gradually add remaining 2 tablespoons sugar, beating until stiff peaks form. Gradually pour chocolate batter over beaten egg whites, folding with rubber spatula just until blended. Pour batter into prepared pan.

▼ Bake 50 to 60 minutes or until top springs back when touched lightly. Immediately invert pan on heat-proof funnel. Cool completely.

▼ Meanwhile, prepare Peanut Butter Filling. Loosen cake from pan; invert onto serving plate. Slice cake horizontally into three layers. Spread about ¾ cup filling between layers, ending with plain layer on top. Spoon Peanut Butter Glaze over top. Cover; refrigerate until just before serving.
12 to 16 servings.

▼ PEANUT BUTTER FILLING: In small saucepan, combine marshmallows, peanut butter chips and milk; cook over medium heat, stirring constantly, until marshmallows and chips are melted and mixture is smooth. Cool to lukewarm. In small mixer bowl, beat whipping cream and vanilla until stiff; fold in peanut butter mixture. Refrigerate 10 minutes or until mixture begins to set.
About 1½ cups filling.

▼ PEANUT BUTTER GLAZE: In small saucepan, combine peanut butter chips and milk. Cook over low heat, stirring constantly, until chips are melted. Gradually add powdered sugar and vanilla; beat or whisk until of spreading consistency (additional milk may be needed).
About ⅔ cup glaze.

Peanutty Chocolate Chiffon Cake

CHOCOLATE CHIP BERRY SHORTCAKE

2 cups all-purpose biscuit
   baking mix
⅓ cup sugar
1 egg
½ cup milk
2 tablespoons vegetable oil
½ cup HERSHEY'S MINI
   CHIPS Semi-Sweet Chocolate
Sweetened whipped cream
4 cups (1 qt.) fresh strawberries,
   sliced and sweetened

▼ Heat oven to 375°F. Grease 8-inch round baking pan. In medium bowl, stir together baking mix and sugar.

▼ In second bowl, slightly beat egg; blend in milk and oil. Add to dry ingredients; stir just until moistened (batter may be lumpy). Stir in small chocolate chips. Spoon batter into prepared pan.

▼ Bake 25 to 30 minutes or until wooden pick inserted in center comes out clean. Cool 10 minutes; remove from pan. Place on serving plate. Cut into wedges; top with sweetened whipped cream and strawberries. *8 servings.*

Chocolate Chip Berry Shortcake

⨍UPREME CHOCOLATE ALMOND TORTE

3 eggs
1¼ cups sugar
1 cup (2 sticks) butter or
margarine, melted
1 teaspoon vanilla extract
Dash salt
½ cup HERSHEY'S European
Style Cocoa
⅓ cup all-purpose flour
¾ cup toasted almonds,
very finely chopped
Supreme Cocoa Glaze

Supreme Cocoa Glaze
2 tablespoons butter or
margarine
2 tablespoons HERSHEY'S
European Style Cocoa
2 tablespoons water
1 cup powdered sugar
½ teaspoon vanilla extract

▼ Heat oven to 350°F. Line 9-inch round baking pan with foil; butter bottom only. In large mixer bowl, beat eggs, sugar, butter, vanilla and salt; beat on high speed of electric mixer 3 minutes until smooth and thick, scraping bowl often.

▼ Add cocoa and flour; blend well. Stir in almonds. Spread batter into prepared pan.

▼ Bake 35 to 40 minutes or until wooden pick inserted in center comes out clean. Cool on wire rack 15 minutes; remove from pan. Carefully peel off foil; cool completely.

▼ Place on serving plate. Spread Supreme Cocoa Glaze over top and sides; garnish with sliced almonds, if desired.
10 to 12 servings.

▼ SUPREME COCOA GLAZE: In small saucepan over low heat, melt butter; add cocoa and water, stirring constantly until mixture thickens. Do not boil. Remove from heat; gradually add powdered sugar and vanilla, beating with spoon until smooth. Add additional water, ½ teaspoon at a time, until desired consistency.
About ¾ cup glaze.

1 To prepare Sweetened Whipped Cream: Pour very cold heavy or whipping cream into small, deep bowl. Add flavoring and powdered sugar.

2 Beat cream mixture with a mixer or wire whisk until stiff.

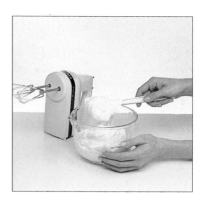

3 Whipped cream is finished when it mounds on a spoon or spatula.

CHOCOLATE BANANA SNACKING CAKE

1²⁄₃ cups all-purpose flour
1 cup packed light brown sugar
¼ cup HERSHEY'S Cocoa
1 teaspoon baking soda
½ teaspoon salt
½ cup water
½ cup mashed ripe banana
   (1 large)
⅓ cup vegetable oil
1 teaspoon white vinegar
½ teaspoon vanilla extract
Whipped topping (optional)

▼ Heat oven to 350°F. In large bowl, stir together flour, brown sugar, cocoa, baking soda and salt. Add water, banana, oil, vinegar and vanilla; stir until smooth. Pour batter into ungreased 8-inch square baking pan.

▼ Bake 35 to 40 minutes or until wooden pick inserted in center comes out clean. Serve warm or cool with whipped topping, if desired.
9 servings.

CHOCOLATE CHIP SNACK CAKE

3 cups all-purpose flour
2 cups sugar
⅔ cup HERSHEY'S Cocoa
2 teaspoons baking soda
1 teaspoon salt
2 cups water
⅔ cup vegetable oil
2 eggs
2 tablespoons white vinegar
2 teaspoons vanilla extract
1 cup HERSHEY'S Semi-Sweet
   Chocolate Chips
Cream Cheese Filling
½ cup chopped nuts

Cream Cheese Filling
1 package (8 oz.) cream cheese,
   softened
⅓ cup sugar
1 egg
½ teaspoon vanilla extract
1 cup HERSHEY'S Semi-Sweet
   Chocolate Chips

▼ Heat oven to 350°F. Grease and flour bottom of 13 x 9 x 2-inch baking pan. In large mixer bowl, stir together flour, sugar, cocoa, baking soda and salt.

▼ Add water, oil, eggs, vinegar and vanilla; beat on medium speed of electric mixer 2 minutes or until well combined. Stir in chocolate chips.

▼ Pour batter into prepared pan. Spoon heaping teaspoonfuls Cream Cheese Filling evenly over batter. Sprinkle nuts over top.

▼ Bake 50 to 55 minutes or until wooden pick inserted in center comes out clean. Cool in pan on wire rack. Cover; store leftover cake in refrigerator.
12 to 16 servings.

▼ CREAM CHEESE FILLING: In small bowl, stir together cream cheese, sugar, egg and vanilla; beat until smooth. Stir in chocolate chips.

COCOA SPICE SNACKING CAKE

¼ **cup (½ stick) butter or
margarine, melted**
¼ **cup HERSHEY'S Cocoa**
¾ **cup applesauce**
1 **cup all-purpose flour**
1 **cup granulated sugar**
¾ **teaspoon baking soda**
½ **teaspoon ground cinnamon**
¼ **teaspoon ground nutmeg**
¼ **teaspoon salt**
1 **egg, slightly beaten**
½ **cup chopped nuts**
½ **cup raisins**
Powdered sugar (optional)

▼ Heat oven to 350°F. Grease 9-inch square baking pan. In small bowl, combine butter and cocoa, stirring until smooth; stir in applesauce.

▼ Stir together flour, sugar, baking soda, cinnamon, nutmeg and salt. Add cocoa mixture and egg; stir until dry ingredients are moistened. Stir in nuts and raisins. Spread batter into prepared pan.

▼ Bake 28 to 30 minutes or until wooden pick inserted in center comes out clean. Cool in pan on wire rack. Sprinkle powdered sugar over top, if desired.
9 servings.

Chocolate Chip Snack Cake, Chocolate Banana Snacking Cake, Cocoa Spice Snacking Cake

CHOCOLATE PEPPERMINT TORTE

2 cups sugar
1¾ cups all-purpose flour
¾ cup HERSHEY'S Cocoa
1½ teaspoons baking powder
1½ teaspoons baking soda
1 teaspoon salt
2 eggs
1 cup milk
½ cup vegetable oil
2 teaspoons vanilla extract
1 cup boiling water
Peppermint Filling
Cocoa Glaze

Peppermint Filling
1½ cups cold whipping cream
½ cup powdered sugar
⅔ cup finely crushed hard
   peppermint candy or
   ½ teaspoon mint extract
¾ teaspoon vanilla extract
Several drops red food color

Cocoa Glaze
2 tablespoons butter or
   margarine
2 tablespoons HERSHEY'S
   Cocoa
2 tablespoons water
1 cup powdered sugar
½ teaspoon vanilla extract

▼ Heat oven to 350°F. Grease and flour three 9-inch round baking pans. In large mixer bowl, stir together dry ingredients.

▼ Add eggs, milk, oil and vanilla; beat on medium speed of electric mixer 2 minutes. Stir in boiling water (batter will be thin). Divide batter among prepared pans.

▼ Bake 20 to 25 minutes or until wooden pick inserted in center comes out clean. Cool 10 minutes; remove from pans to wire racks. Cool completely.

▼ Spread Peppermint Filling between layers, reserving ½ cup for garnish. Spread Cocoa Glaze over top of torte. Refrigerate. Before serving, garnish with reserved filling. Cover; refrigerate remaining torte. *10 to 12 servings.*

▼ PEPPERMINT FILLING: In small mixer bowl, beat whipping cream and powdered sugar until stiff. Fold in peppermint candy, vanilla and red food color until evenly blended.
About 3 cups filling.

▼ COCOA GLAZE: In small saucepan over low heat, melt butter; add cocoa and water, stirring constantly until slightly thickened. Remove from heat; gradually add powdered sugar and vanilla, beating with wire whisk until smooth and of spreading consistency. Add additional water, ½ teaspoon at a time, if needed. *About ½ cup glaze.*

Note: If only two pans are available, reserve remaining batter in refrigerator while first two layers bake.

Chocolate Peppermint Torte

DEEP DARK CHOCOLATE CAKE

2 cups sugar
1¾ cups all-purpose flour
¾ cup HERSHEY'S Cocoa or
   HERSHEY'S European Style
   Cocoa
1½ teaspoons baking powder
1½ teaspoons baking soda
1 teaspoon salt
2 eggs
1 cup milk
½ cup vegetable oil
2 teaspoons vanilla extract
1 cup boiling water
One-Bowl Buttercream Frosting

▼ Heat oven to 350°F. Grease and flour two 9-inch round baking pans or one 13 x 9 x 2-inch baking pan.

▼In large mixer bowl, stir together sugar, flour, cocoa, baking powder, baking soda and salt. Add eggs, milk, oil and vanilla; beat on medium speed of electric mixer 2 minutes.

▼ Remove from mixer; stir in boiling water (batter will be thin). Pour batter into prepared pans.

▼ Bake 30 to 35 minutes for round pans, 35 to 40 minutes for rectangular pan or until wooden pick inserted in center comes out clean.

▼ Cool 10 minutes; remove from pans to wire racks. Cool completely. (Cake may be left in rectangular pan, if desired.) Frost with One-Bowl Buttercream Frosting. *8 to 10 servings.*
(continued)

Deep Dark Chocolate Cake

One-Bowl Buttercream Frosting
**6 tablespoons butter or
   margarine, softened**
2⅔ cups powdered sugar
**½ cup HERSHEY'S Cocoa or
   HERSHEY'S European Style
   Cocoa**
⅓ cup milk
1 teaspoon vanilla extract

▼ ONE-BOWL BUTTERCREAM FROSTING: In
small mixer bowl, beat butter. Add powdered sugar
and cocoa alternately with milk; beat to spreading
consistency (additional milk may be needed). Blend
in vanilla.
About 2 cups frosting.

*E*UROPEAN MOCHA FUDGE CAKE

**1¼ cups (2½ sticks) butter or
   margarine**
**¾ cup HERSHEY'S European
   Style Cocoa**
4 eggs
¼ teaspoon salt
1 teaspoon vanilla extract
2 cups sugar
1 cup all-purpose flour
1 cup finely chopped pecans
Creamy Coffee Filling
Chocolate curls (optional)

Creamy Coffee Filling
1½ cups cold whipping cream
**⅓ cup packed light brown
   sugar**
**½ to 1 teaspoon powdered
   instant coffee**

▼ Heat oven to 350°F. Butter bottom and sides of
two 9-inch round baking pans. Line bottoms with
wax paper; butter paper. In small saucepan, melt
butter; remove from heat. Stir in cocoa, blending
well; cool slightly.

▼ In large mixer bowl, beat eggs until foamy; add salt
and vanilla. Gradually add sugar, beating well. Add
cooled chocolate mixture; blend thoroughly. Fold in
flour. Stir in pecans. Pour batter into prepared pans.

▼ Bake 20 to 25 minutes or until wooden pick inserted
in center comes out clean. Do not overbake. Cool
5 minutes; remove from pans. Carefully peel off
paper. Cool completely.

▼ Spread Creamy Coffee Filling between layers, over
top and sides of cake. Garnish with chocolate curls, if
desired. Refrigerate 1 hour or longer before serving.
10 to 12 servings.

▼ CREAMY COFFEE FILLING: In small mixer bowl,
combine all ingredients; stir until coffee is almost
dissolved. Beat until stiff.
About 3 cups filling.

▼ MAKE AHEAD DIRECTIONS: Cooled cake may
be wrapped and frozen up to 4 weeks; thaw,
wrapped, before filling and frosting.

BLACK FOREST CAKE

1²/₃ cups all-purpose flour
1½ cups sugar
½ cup HERSHEY'S Cocoa
1½ teaspoons baking soda
1 teaspoon salt
½ teaspoon baking powder
2 eggs
½ cup shortening
1½ cups buttermilk or
　sour milk*
1 teaspoon vanilla extract
Sweetened Whipped Cream
1 can (21 oz.) cherry pie filling
Sliced almonds

Sweetened Whipped Cream
1½ cups cold whipping cream
3 tablespoons powdered sugar
¾ teaspoon vanilla extract

▼ Heat oven to 350°F. Grease and flour two 9-inch round baking pans. In large mixer bowl, stir together flour, sugar, cocoa, baking soda, salt and baking powder; add eggs, shortening, buttermilk and vanilla.

▼ Beat on low speed of electric mixer 1 minute, scraping bowl constantly. Beat on high speed 3 minutes, scraping bowl occasionally. Pour batter into prepared pans.

▼ Bake 30 to 35 minutes or until wooden pick inserted in center comes out clean. Cool 10 minutes; remove from pans to wire racks. Cool completely.

▼ Prepare Sweetened Whipped Cream. Place one cake layer on serving plate. Spoon one-half of pie filling in center and spread to within ½ inch of edge. Spoon or pipe border of whipped cream around edge. Top with second layer. Spoon remaining pie filling to within ½ inch of edge.

▼ Frost sides with whipped cream; spoon or pipe border around top edge. Pat almonds onto sides of cake. Refrigerate until serving time. Refrigerate leftover cake.
10 to 12 servings.

▼ SWEETENED WHIPPED CREAM: In small mixer bowl, combine whipping cream, powdered sugar and vanilla; beat until stiff.
About 3 cups.

* To sour milk: Use 4½ teaspoons white vinegar plus milk to equal 1½ cups.

CHOCOLATE GLAZED CITRUS POPPY SEED CAKE

1 package (about 18.25 oz.) lemon cake mix
⅓ cup poppy seed
⅓ cup milk
3 eggs
1 container (8 oz.) plain lowfat yogurt
1 teaspoon freshly grated lemon peel
Chocolate Citrus Glaze

Chocolate Citrus Glaze
2 tablespoons butter or margarine
2 tablespoons HERSHEY'S European Style Cocoa or HERSHEY'S Cocoa
2 tablespoons water
1 tablespoon orange flavored liqueur (optional)
½ teaspoon orange extract
1¼ to 1½ cups powdered sugar

▼ Heat oven to 350°F. Grease and flour 12-cup fluted tube pan or 10-inch tube pan. In large mixer bowl, combine cake mix, poppy seed, milk, eggs, yogurt and lemon peel; beat until well blended. Pour batter into prepared pan.

▼ Bake 40 to 45 minutes or until wooden pick inserted in center comes out clean. Cool 20 minutes; remove from pan to wire rack. Cool completely.

▼ Spoon Chocolate Citrus Glaze over cake, allowing to drip down sides.
12 servings.

▼ CHOCOLATE CITRUS GLAZE : In small saucepan over medium heat, melt butter. With wire whisk, stir in cocoa and water until mixture thickens slightly. Remove from heat; stir in liqueur, if desired, orange extract and 1¼ cups powdered sugar. Whisk until smooth. If glaze is too thin, whisk in remaining ¼ cup powdered sugar. Use immediately.

Chocolate Glazed Citrus Poppy Cake

QUICK 'N' EASY CHOCOLATE CUPCAKES

2 cups all-purpose flour
1½ cups sugar
⅔ cup HERSHEY'S Cocoa
2 teaspoons baking powder
½ teaspoon baking soda
½ teaspoon salt
⅔ cup shortening
2 eggs
⅔ cup milk
½ cup hot water
1½ teaspoons vanilla extract
Creamy Fudge Frosting

Creamy Fudge Frosting
½ cup (1 stick) butter or
    margarine
½ cup HERSHEY'S Cocoa
3⅔ cups (1 lb.) powdered sugar
1½ teaspoons vanilla extract
Dash salt
⅓ cup water

▼ Heat oven to 350°F. Paper-line 30 muffin cups (2½ inches in diameter). In large mixer bowl, stir together flour, sugar, cocoa, baking powder, baking soda and salt.

▼ Add shortening, eggs, milk, water and vanilla; beat on low speed of electric mixer 1 minute. Beat on medium speed additional 3 minutes or until mixture is smooth and creamy. Spoon batter into prepared cups, filling each cup about one-half full.

▼ Bake 15 to 20 minutes or until center of cupcake springs back when touched lightly in center. Remove cupcakes from pan to wire rack.

▼ Cool completely. (Do not cool cupcakes in pan; paper liners will come loose from cupcakes.) Prepare Creamy Fudge Frosting. Frost cooled cupcakes. *30 cupcakes.*

▼ CREAMY FUDGE FROSTING: In medium saucepan over low heat, melt butter. Add cocoa; stir until smooth and well blended. Remove from heat. Add powdered sugar, vanilla and salt alternately with water; beat with spoon or wire whisk until smooth and creamy. Additional water, ½ teaspoon at a time, may be added, if frosting becomes too thick. *About 2 cups frosting.*

1 Dress up a chocolate cake by placing a clean pre-cut stencil over a flat cake surface.

2 Gently sift powdered sugar over cake being careful to not get sugar outside stencil.

3 Carefully remove stencil.

ONE BOWL CHOCOLATE CAKE

⅔ cup butter or margarine, softened
1¾ cups sugar
2 cups all-purpose flour
½ cup HERSHEY'S Cocoa
2 teaspoons baking powder
½ teaspoon baking soda
½ teaspoon salt
3 eggs
1½ cups milk
1 teaspoon vanilla extract

▼ Heat oven to 350°F. Grease and flour two 8- or 9-inch round baking pans or one 13 x 9 x 2-inch baking pan. In large mixer bowl, beat butter and sugar until well blended. Add remaining ingredients.

▼ Beat on low speed of electric mixer 1 minute, scraping bowl constantly. Beat on high speed 2 minutes, scraping bowl and beaters occasionally. Pour batter into prepared pans.

▼ Bake 30 to 35 minutes for round pans, 40 to 45 minutes for rectangular pan or until wooden pick inserted in center comes out clean. Cool 10 minutes; remove from pans to wire racks. Cool completely. (Cake may be left in rectangular pan, if desired.) Frost as desired.
8 to 12 servings.

Quick 'n' Easy Chocolate Cupcakes, One Bowl Chocolate Cake

Chocolate Ice Cream Cake

CHOCOLATE ICE CREAM CAKE

2 eggs, separated
1½ cups sugar, divided
1¼ cups all-purpose flour
½ cup HERSHEY'S Cocoa
¾ teaspoon baking soda
½ teaspoon salt
½ cup vegetable oil
1 cup buttermilk or sour milk*
Ice Cream Layers
¾ cup sweetened whipped cream
　or non-dairy whipped topping
½ cup fresh fruit, sliced
Chocolate Rosettes (optional, see
　page 178)

Ice Cream Layers
½ gallon of your favorite flavor
　ice cream, slightly softened

▼ Heat oven to 350°F. Grease and flour three 9-inch round baking pans. In small mixer bowl, beat egg whites until foamy; gradually add ½ cup sugar, beating until stiff peaks form. Set aside.

▼ In large mixer bowl, stir together flour, remaining 1 cup sugar, cocoa, baking soda and salt. Add oil, buttermilk and egg yolks; beat until smooth. Gently fold egg white mixture into batter. Pour about 1⅔ cups batter into each prepared pan.

▼ Bake 18 to 20 minutes or until cake springs back when touched lightly in center. Cool 5 minutes; remove from pans to wire racks.

▼ Cool completely. Wrap each layer separately in foil; freeze several hours or several days in advance of serving.

▼ Prepare Ice Cream Layers. Remove cake and Ice Cream Layers from freezer; peel off foil. On serving plate, alternately layer cake and ice cream layers, beginning and ending with cake. Wrap tightly; return to freezer.

▼ Just before serving, frost top of cake with whipped cream. Arrange fruit in decorative design on top; pipe on Chocolate Rosettes, if desired.
10 to 12 servings.

▼ ICE CREAM LAYERS: Line two 9-inch round layer pans with foil; working quickly, evenly spread ice cream into prepared pans. Cover tightly; freeze until firm.

* To sour milk: Use 1 tablespoon white vinegar plus milk to equal 1 cup.

FRESH APPLE MINI CHIP CAKE

3 eggs
1 cup vegetable oil
1/2 cup bottled apple juice
2 teaspoons vanilla extract
3 cups all-purpose flour
1 3/4 cups sugar
1 teaspoon baking soda
3/4 teaspoon salt
1/2 teaspoon ground cinnamon
3 cups diced, peeled tart apples
1 cup HERSHEY'S MINI CHIPS
   Semi-Sweet Chocolate
3/4 cup finely chopped nuts
Cream Cheese Frosting
Additional HERSHEY'S MINI
   CHIPS Semi-Sweet Chocolate
   (optional)

Cream Cheese Frosting
1 package (3 oz.) cream cheese,
   softened
2 tablespoons butter or
   magarine, softened
2 cups powdered sugar
1 teaspoon vanilla extract

▼ Heat oven to 350°F. Grease and flour two 9-inch round baking pans.* In large bowl, beat eggs slightly; stir in oil, apple juice and vanilla.

▼ Stir together flour, sugar, baking soda, salt and cinnamon; stir into egg mixture until smooth. Add apples, 1 cup small chocolate chips and nuts; stir until mixed evenly. Pour batter into prepared pans.

▼ Bake 40 to 45 minutes or until wooden pick inserted in center comes out clean. Cool 10 minutes; remove from pans to wire racks. Cool completely.

▼ Prepare Cream Cheese Frosting. Spread one-half frosting on bottom layer; top with second layer. Spread remaining frosting on top of cake. Garnish with additional small chocolate chips, if desired. *10 to 12 servings.*

▼ CREAM CHEESE FROSTING: In small mixer bowl, beat cream cheese and butter until smooth and well blended. Gradually add powdered sugar; stir in vanilla. Beat until smooth. (1 to 2 teaspoons milk may be added for desired spreading consistency.) *About 1 cup frosting.*

* Cake may also be baked in well greased and floured 13 x 9 x 2-inch baking pan 35 to 40 minutes.

CHOCOLATEY FRESH APPLE CAKE

2 3/4 cups all-purpose flour
2 cups granulated sugar
2/3 cup HERSHEY'S Cocoa
1 1/2 teaspoons baking soda
1/2 teaspoon baking powder
1 teaspoon ground cinnamon
3/4 teaspoon salt
3 eggs
1 cup buttermilk or sour milk*
1 cup vegetable oil
2 teaspoons vanilla extract

▼ Heat oven to 350°F. Grease and flour 12-cup fluted tube pan. Stir together flour, granulated sugar, cocoa, baking soda, baking powder, cinnamon and salt; set aside.

▼ In large mixer bowl, combine eggs, buttermilk, oil and vanilla; beat on low speed of electric mixer until blended. Gradually add dry ingredients; stir in apples and nuts until mixed evenly. Pour batter into prepared pan.
(continued)

2 cups shredded tart apples,
  drained**
1 cup finely chopped nuts
Powdered sugar or Chocolate
  Glaze

Chocolate Glaze
2 tablespoons butter or
  margarine
2 tablespoons HERSHEY'S
  Cocoa
2 tablespoons water
1 cup powdered sugar
1 teaspoon vanilla extract

▼ Bake 1 hour to 1 hour and 5 minutes or until wooden pick inserted in center of cake comes out clean. Cool 10 minutes.

▼ Remove from pan to wire rack. Cool completely. Sprinkle top with powdered sugar or drizzle with Chocolate Glaze.
10 to 12 servings.

▼ CHOCOLATE GLAZE: In small saucepan over low heat, melt butter. Add cocoa and water, stirring constantly until mixture thickens. Do not boil. Remove from heat; gradually beat in powdered sugar and vanilla until smooth and of glazing consistency. Add additional water, ½ teaspoon at a time, if necessary.
About ½ cup glaze.

* To sour milk: Use 1 tablespoon white vinegar plus milk to equal 1 cup.

** Shred in food processor, if available.

Chocolatey Fresh Apple Cake, Fresh Apple Mini Chip Cake

HEAVENLY CHOCOLATE MOUSSE FILLED CAKE

1 package (about 15 oz.) "two-
    step" angel food cake mix
3 to 4 drops red food color
Chocolate Mousse Filling
Whipped Cream Frosting
Chocolate Hearts (optional,
    see page 176)

Chocolate Mousse Filling
1 envelope unflavored gelatin
2 tablespoons cold water
¼ cup boiling water
⅔ cup sugar
⅓ cup HERSHEY'S Cocoa
1½ cups cold whipping cream
2 teaspoons vanilla extract

Whipped Cream Frosting
1 cup (½ pt.) cold whipping
    cream
¼ cup powdered sugar
1 teaspoon vanilla extract
2 to 3 drops red food color

▼ Move oven rack to lowest position. Mix cake as directed on package, adding food color to stiffly beaten egg white mixture.

▼ Bake and cool as directed for 10-inch tube pan. Place cake on serving plate, rounded side down. Using serrated knife, cut 1-inch layer from top of cake; lift off in one piece. Set aside.

▼ Using serrated knife, cut trench in cake 1 inch wide and 1½ inches deep, leaving 1-inch-wide inner and outer walls of cake. Using a fork, carefully remove cake in trench without breaking through sides or bottom. Prepare Chocolate Mousse Filling; spoon into cake shell. Replace top of cake.

▼ Frost cake with Whipped Cream Frosting. Refrigerate at least 1 hour before serving. Garnish with Chocolate Hearts. Refrigerate leftover cake. *12 to 16 servings.*

▼ CHOCOLATE MOUSSE FILLING: In small bowl, sprinkle gelatin over cold water; let stand 1 minute to soften. Add boiling water; stir until gelatin is completely dissolved and mixture is clear. Cool slightly. In small mixer bowl, stir together sugar and cocoa; add whipping cream and vanilla. Beat on medium speed of electric mixer, scraping bottom of bowl occasionally, until stiff. Pour in gelatin mixture; beat until well blended. *About 3 cups filling.*

▼ WHIPPED CREAM FROSTING: In small mixer bowl, combine whipping cream, powdered sugar, vanilla and food color; beat until stiff. *About 2 cups frosting.*

Heavenly Chocolate Mousse Filled Cake

RED VELVET COCOA CAKE

Red Velvet Cocoa Cake

½ cup (1 stick) butter or
  margarine, softened
1½ cups sugar
1 teaspoon vanilla extract
2 eggs
1 tablespoon red food color
2 cups all-purpose flour
¼ cup HERSHEY'S Cocoa
1 teaspoon salt
1 cup buttermilk or sour milk*
1½ teaspoons baking soda
1 tablespoon white vinegar
Fluffy Vanilla Frosting

▼ Heat oven to 350°F. Grease and flour two 9-inch round baking pans. In large mixer bowl, beat butter, sugar and vanilla until creamy. Add eggs and food color; blend well.

▼ Stir together flour, cocoa and salt; add alternately with buttermilk to butter mixture, beating until well blended. Stir baking soda into vinegar; fold carefully into batter (do not beat). Pour batter into prepared pans.

▼ Bake 30 to 35 minutes or until wooden pick inserted in center comes out clean. Cool 10 minutes; remove from pans to wire racks. Cool completely. Frost with Fluffy Vanilla Frosting.
10 to 12 servings.
(continued)

Fluffy Vanilla Frosting
**½ cup (1 stick) butter or
    margarine, softened
5 cups powdered sugar, divided
2 teaspoons vanilla extract
⅛ teaspoon salt
4 to 5 tablespoons milk**

▼ FLUFFY VANILLA FROSTING: In large mixer bowl, beat butter, 1 cup powdered sugar, vanilla and salt until well blended. Add remaining 4 cups powdered sugar alternately with milk, beating to spreading consistency.
About 2 ¾ cups frosting.

* To sour milk: Use 1 tablespoon white vinegar plus milk to equal 1 cup.

$\mathcal{T}$RIPLE LAYER CHOCOLATE MOUSSE CAKE

**2 cups sugar
1¾ cups all-purpose flour
¾ cup HERSHEY'S Cocoa or
    HERSHEY'S European
    Style Cocoa
1½ teaspoons baking powder
1½ teaspoons baking soda
1 teaspoon salt
2 eggs
1 cup milk
½ cup vegetable oil
2 teaspoons vanilla extract
1 cup boiling water
Chocolate Mousse
Sliced almonds (optional)
Chocolate curls (optional)**

Chocolate Mousse
**1 envelope unflavored gelatin
2 tablespoons cold water
¼ cup boiling water
1 cup sugar
½ cup HERSHEY'S Cocoa
2 cups (1 pt.) cold
    whipping cream
2 teaspoons vanilla extract**

▼ Heat oven to 350°F. Grease and flour three 8-inch round baking pans. In large mixer bowl, stir together sugar, flour, cocoa, baking powder, baking soda and salt.

▼ Add eggs, milk, oil and vanilla; beat on medium speed of electric mixer 2 minutes. Remove from mixer; stir in boiling water (batter will be thin). Pour batter into prepared pans.

▼ Bake 30 to 35 minutes or until wooden pick inserted in center comes out clean. Cool 10 minutes; remove from pans to wire racks. Cool completely.

▼ Prepare Chocolate Mousse. Fill and frost layers with mousse. Garnish with almonds and chocolate curls, if desired. Refrigerate at least 1 hour. Cover; refrigerate leftover cake.
10 to 12 servings.

▼ CHOCOLATE MOUSSE: In small bowl, sprinkle gelatin over cold water; let stand 1 minute to soften. Add boiling water; stir until gelatin is completely dissolved and mixture is clear. Cool slightly. In large cold mixer bowl, stir together sugar and cocoa; add whipping cream and vanilla. Beat on medium speed of electric mixer, scraping bottom of bowl occasionally, until stiff; pour in gelatin mixture and beat until well blended. Refrigerate about ½ hour.
About 4 cups.

CHOCOLATE ALMOND CHEESECAKE

3 packages (8 oz. each) cream cheese, softened
1¼ cups sugar
⅓ cup HERSHEY'S Cocoa
½ cup dairy sour cream
2 tablespoons all-purpose flour
3 eggs
2 teaspoons almond extract
1 teaspoon vanilla extract
Almond Crumb Crust
Almond Whipped Cream
Sliced almonds (optional)

Almond Crumb Crust
¾ cup (about 20 wafers) vanilla wafer crumbs
½ cup ground blanched almonds
3 tablespoons sugar
3 tablespoons butter or margarine, melted

Almond Whipped Cream
½ cup cold whipping cream
2 tablespoons powdered sugar
¼ teaspoon vanilla extract
⅛ teaspoon almond extract

▼ Heat oven to 425°F. In large mixer bowl, combine cream cheese, sugar, cocoa, sour cream and flour; beat on medium speed of electric mixer until smooth. Add eggs and almond and vanilla extracts; beat well. Pour into prepared Almond Crumb Crust.

▼ Bake 10 minutes. Reduce oven temperature to 250°F; continue baking 55 minutes or until center appears set. Remove from oven to wire rack.

▼ With knife, loosen cake from side of pan. Cool completely; remove side of pan. Refrigerate several hours or overnight.

▼ Garnish with Almond Whipped Cream and sliced almonds, if desired. Cover; refrigerate leftover cheesecake.
10 to 12 servings.

▼ ALMOND CRUMB CRUST: Heat oven to 350°F. In small bowl, stir together vanilla wafer crumbs, almonds and sugar; stir in butter, mixing well. Press mixture onto bottom and ½ inch up side of 9-inch springform pan. Bake 8 to 10 minutes; cool slightly.

▼ ALMOND WHIPPED CREAM: In small mixer bowl, combine cold whipping cream, powdered sugar, vanilla and almond extracts; beat until stiff.
About 1 cup cream.

1 Coarsely chop vanilla wafers and almonds in food processor. Mix together all crust ingredients.

2 Press crust mixture firmly onto bottom and side of spring-form pan.

3 Pour cheesecake batter into prepared crust.

Chocolate Almond Cheesecake

Vanilla Citrus Cheesecake

2 cups graham cracker crumbs
1/3 cup butter or margarine, melted
2 tablespoons plus 1½ cups sugar, divided
3 packages (8 oz. each) cream cheese, softened
4 eggs
1 teaspoon vanilla extract
1 teaspoon freshly grated orange peel
1⅔ cups (10-oz. pkg.) HERSHEY'S Vanilla Milk Chips
Chocolate Drizzle

Chocolate Drizzle
½ cup HERSHEY'S Semi-Sweet Chocolate Chips
1 tablespoon shortening (do not use butter, margarine, or oil)

▼ Heat oven to 350°F. In small bowl, stir together crumbs, butter and 2 tablespoons sugar. Press mixture evenly onto bottom of 9-inch springform pan. Bake 5 minutes or just until golden brown; remove from oven (do not turn off oven).

▼ In large mixer bowl, beat cream cheese and remaining 1½ cups sugar until smooth. Add eggs, vanilla extract and orange peel; beat well.

▼ In small microwave-safe bowl, place vanilla milk chips. Microwave at HIGH (100%) 1 to 1½ minutes or until chips are melted and smooth when stirred vigorously. Blend into cream cheese mixture. Pour over crust.

▼ Bake 35 to 40 minutes or just until almost set. Remove from oven to wire rack. With knife, loosen cake from side of pan. Cool completely; remove side of pan.

▼ Refrigerate until firm. Using tip of spoon, drizzle Chocolate Drizzle across top of cheesecake. Cover; refrigerate leftover cheesecake.
10 to 12 servings.

▼ CHOCOLATE DRIZZLE: In small microwave-safe bowl, place chocolate chips and shortening. Microwave at HIGH (100%) 30 to 45 seconds or until chocolate is melted and mixture is smooth when stirred.

Chocolate Festival Cheesecake

3 packages (8 oz. each) cream cheese, softened
1¼ cups sugar
¼ cup HERSHEY'S Cocoa
½ cup dairy sour cream
2 teaspoons vanilla extract
2 tablespoons all-purpose flour
3 eggs
Chocolate Crumb Crust

▼ Heat oven to 450°F. In large mixer bowl, combine cream cheese, sugar, cocoa, sour cream and vanilla; beat on medium speed of electric mixer until smooth. Add flour and eggs; beat well. Pour into prepared Chocolate Crumb Crust.

▼ Bake 10 minutes. Without opening oven, reduce temperature to 250°F; continue baking 30 minutes. (Cheesecake may not appear set in middle.)
(continued)

Chocolate curls (optional, see page 177)
Assorted fresh fruit, sliced (optional)
Sweetened whipped cream or whipped topping (optional)

Chocolate Crumb Crust
1¼ cups (about 40 wafers) vanilla wafer crumbs
⅓ cup powdered sugar
⅓ cup HERSHEY'S Cocoa
¼ cup (½ stick) butter or margarine, melted

▼ Turn off oven; leave cheesecake in oven 30 minutes without opening door. Remove from oven. With knife, loosen cake from side of pan. Cool to room temperature; remove side of pan.

▼ Refrigerate several hours or overnight. Garnish with chocolate curls or sliced fruit and whipped cream, if desired. Cover; refrigerate leftover cheesecake. *10 to 12 servings.*

▼ CHOCOLATE CRUMB CRUST: Heat oven to 350°F. In small bowl, stir together vanilla wafer crumbs, powdered sugar and cocoa; stir in butter. Press mixture onto bottom and ½ inch up side of 9-inch springform pan. Bake 8 to 10 minutes. Cool.

Chocolate Festival Cheesecake

GERMAN CHOCOLATE CHEESECAKE

4 bars (4 oz.) HERSHEY'S Semi-Sweet Baking Chocolate, broken into pieces

3 packages (8 oz. each) cream cheese, softened

¾ cup sugar

½ cup dairy sour cream

2 teaspoons vanilla extract

2 tablespoons all-purpose flour

3 eggs

Coconut-Pecan Graham Crust

Coconut Pecan Topping

Coconut-Pecan Graham Crust

1 cup graham cracker crumbs

2 tablespoons sugar

⅓ cup butter or margarine, melted

¼ cup flaked coconut

¼ cup chopped pecans

Coconut-Pecan Topping

½ cup (1 stick) butter or margarine

¼ cup packed light brown sugar

2 tablespoons light cream

2 tablespoons light corn syrup

1 cup flaked coconut

½ cup chopped pecans

1 teaspoon vanilla extract

▼ Heat oven to 450°F. In small microwave-safe bowl, place chocolate. Microwave at HIGH (100%) 1 to 1½ minutes or until chocolate is melted and smooth when stirred; set aside.

▼ In large mixer bowl, combine cream cheese, sugar, sour cream and vanilla; beat on medium speed of electric mixer until smooth. Add flour, 1 tablespoon at a time, blending well. Add eggs and reserved chocolate; blend well. Pour into Coconut Pecan Graham Crust.

▼ Bake 10 minutes; without opening oven door, reduce oven temperature to 250°F. Continue baking 35 minutes; remove from oven. With knife, loosen cake from side of pan. Cool completely; remove side of pan.

▼ Prepare Coconut-Pecan Topping. Spread topping over top of cake. Refrigerate until firm.
10 to 12 servings.

▼ COCONUT-PECAN GRAHAM CRUST: Heat oven to 350°F. In small bowl, combine graham cracker crumbs and sugar. Stir in butter, coconut and pecans; mix thoroughly. Press mixture onto bottom and ½ inch up side of 9-inch springform pan. Bake 8 to 10 minutes. Cool.

▼ COCONUT-PECAN TOPPING: In small saucepan, melt butter; add brown sugar, light cream and corn syrup. Cook over medium heat, stirring constantly, until smooth and bubbly. Remove from heat. Stir in coconut, pecans and vanilla. Cool slightly.

CHOCOLATE AMARETTO CHEESECAKE

1 envelope unflavored gelatin
¼ cup cold water
2 containers (8 oz. each)
 soft-style cream cheese
1 cup sugar
½ cup HERSHEY'S Cocoa
2 tablespoons amaretto (almond-
 flavored liqueur) or ¾ teaspoon
 almond extract
1 teaspoon vanilla extract
1 cup (½ pt.) cold whipping
 cream
Coconut-Nut Crust
Sweetened whipped cream
Chocolate curls (optional, see
 page 177)

Coconut-Nut Crust
1 cup coconut cookie crumbs
 (use crisp coconut cookies)
¼ cup ground almonds
¼ cup (½ stick) butter or
 margarine, softened

▼ In small saucepan, sprinkle gelatin over water; let stand 1 minute. Cook over low heat, stirring constantly, until gelatin is completely dissolved, about 3 minutes.

▼ In large mixer bowl, beat cream cheese and sugar on medium speed of electric mixer 2 minutes or until light and fluffy. Add cocoa, liqueur and vanilla; beat until smooth. Gradually add gelatin mixture, beating until thoroughly blended.

▼ In small mixer bowl, beat whipping cream until stiff; fold into chocolate mixture. Pour over prepared Coconut-Nut Crust; refrigerate until firm, about 6 hours. With knife, loosen cake from side of pan; remove side of pan.

▼ Garnish with sweetened whipped cream and chocolate curls, if desired. Cover; refrigerate leftover cheesecake. *10 to 12 servings.*

▼ COCONUT-NUT CRUST: Heat oven to 350°F. In small bowl, stir together coconut cookie crumbs, ground almonds and butter; press mixture onto bottom of 9-inch springform pan.

Chocolate Amaretto Cheesecake

Easy Chocolate Lover's Cheesecake

2 packages (8 oz. each) cream
cheese, softened
½ cup sugar
2 eggs
1 teaspoon vanilla extract
1 cup HERSHEY'S MINI
CHIPS Semi-Sweet Chocolate
1 packaged graham cracker
crumb crust (6 oz.)
Chocolate Topping

Chocolate Topping
⅓ cup HERSHEY'S MINI
CHIPS Semi-Sweet Chocolate
2 tablespoons whipping cream

▼ Heat oven to 450°F. In small mixer bowl, beat cream cheese and sugar until well blended. Add eggs and vanilla; beat well. Stir in small chocolate chips; pour batter into crust.

▼ Bake 10 minutes; without opening door, reduce temperature to 250°F. Continue baking 20 to 25 minutes or just until set. Cool completely.

▼ Cover; refrigerate several hours. Spread Chocolate Topping over top. Refrigerate several minutes or just until set. Cut into wedges; serve cold.
6 servings.

▼ CHOCOLATE TOPPING: In small microwave safe bowl, place small chocolate chips and whipping cream. Microwave at HIGH (100%) 20 to 30 seconds or just until chocolate is melted and mixture is smooth when stirred. Cool slightly.

Simple Chocolate Cheesecakes

24 vanilla wafers
2 packages (8 oz. each) cream
cheese, softened
1¼ cups sugar
⅓ cup HERSHEY'S Cocoa
2 tablespoons all-purpose flour
3 eggs
1 cup (8 oz.) dairy sour cream
1 teaspoon vanilla extract
Sour Cream Topping
Canned cherry pie filling, chilled

Sour Cream Topping
1 cup (8 oz.) dairy sour cream
2 tablespoons sugar
1 teaspoon vanilla extract

▼ Heat oven to 325°F. Line muffin pans (2½ inches in diameter) with foil bake cups. Place one vanilla wafer in bottom of each cup.

▼ In large mixer bowl, beat cream cheese until smooth. Add sugar, cocoa and flour; blend well. Add eggs; beat well. Stir in sour cream and vanilla. Fill each prepared cup almost full with cheese mixture.

▼ Bake 20 to 25 minutes or until set. Remove from oven; cool 5 to 10 minutes. Spread heaping teaspoonful Sour Cream Topping on each cup. Cool completely in pans; refrigerate.

▼ Garnish with dollop of cherry pie filling just before serving. Refrigerate leftover cheesecakes.
About 2 dozen cheesecakes.

▼ SOUR CREAM TOPPING: In small bowl, stir together sour cream, sugar and vanilla; stir until sugar dissolves.

BLACK-EYED SUSAN CHEESECAKES

24 vanilla wafers
2 packages (8 oz. each) cream
   cheese, softened
$\frac{1}{2}$ cup sugar
2 eggs
$\frac{1}{2}$ teaspoon vanilla extract
1 cup REESE'S Peanut Butter
   Chips
$\frac{1}{2}$ cup HERSHEY'S Semi-Sweet
   Chocolate Chips
3 tablespoons butter
Sliced almonds

▼ Heat oven to 350°F. Line muffin pans with foil bake cups (2 inches in diameter). Place one vanilla wafer in bottom of each cup.

▼ In large mixer bowl, beat cream cheese and sugar. Add eggs and vanilla; beat well. Stir in peanut butter chips. Spoon heaping tablespoonful cream cheese mixture into each cup.

▼ Bake 15 minutes or just until set, but not browned. Cool in pans on wire rack.

▼ In small microwave-safe bowl, place chocolate chips and butter. Microwave at HIGH (100%) 30 seconds to 1 minute or until chips are melted and mixture is smooth when stirred.

▼ Drop teaspoonfuls of chocolate mixture onto center of each cheesecake, letting white show around edge. Place almond slices around chocolate mixture to resemble petals. Cover; refrigerate.
About 2 dozen cheesecakes.

Black-Eyed Susan Cheesecakes, Simple Chocolate Cheesecakes

RASPBERRY CHOCOLATE SWIRL CHEESECAKE

Raspberry Chocolate Swirl Cheesecake

3 packages (8 oz. each) cream cheese, softened
1 cup sugar, divided
1½ teaspoons vanilla extract, divided
3 eggs
¼ cup HERSHEY'S Cocoa
1 tablespoon vegetable oil
⅔ cup seedless red raspberry jam
3 tablespoons all-purpose flour
3 to 4 drops red food color (optional)

▼ Heat oven to 425°F. In large mixer bowl, beat cream cheese, ¾ cup sugar and 1 teaspoon vanilla until smooth. Add eggs; beat until well blended.

▼ In small bowl, stir together cocoa and remaining ¼ cup sugar. Add oil, remaining ½ teaspoon vanilla and 1½ cups cream cheese mixture; blend well.

▼ Stir raspberry jam to soften. Add jam, flour and food color, if desired, to remaining mixture in bowl; blend well.
(continued)

Chocolate Crumb Crust
Raspberry Sauce
Raspberries (optional)

Chocolate Crumb Crust
1¼ cups (about 40 wafers)
vanilla wafer crumbs
¼ cup HERSHEY'S Cocoa
¼ cup powdered sugar
¼ cup (½ stick) butter or
margarine, melted

Raspberry Sauce
¼ cup sugar
2 teaspoons cornstarch
1 package (10 oz.) frozen red
raspberries, thawed

▼ Pour half of raspberry mixture into crust; dollop about half of chocolate mixture onto raspberry. Repeat procedure with remaining mixture, ending with chocolate dollops on top; gently swirl with knife or metal spatula for marbled effect.

▼ Bake 10 minutes. Reduce oven temperature to 250°F; continue baking 55 minutes or until center appears set. Remove from oven to wire rack.

▼ With knife, loosen cake from side of pan. Cool completely; remove side of pan. Cover; refrigerate.

▼ Serve with Raspberry Sauce and raspberries, if desired. Cover; refrigerate leftover cheesecake. *10 to 12 servings.*

▼ CHOCOLATE CRUMB CRUST: Heat oven to 350°F. In medium bowl, stir together vanilla wafer crumbs, cocoa and powdered sugar. Stir in butter. Press mixture onto bottom and ½ inch up side of 9-inch springform pan. Bake 8 to 10 minutes; cool slightly.

▼ RASPBERRY SAUCE: In small saucepan, stir together sugar and cornstarch; stir in raspberries. Heat to boiling, stirring constantly; boil and stir 1 minute. Cool; press through sieve to remove seeds. *About 1 cup sauce.*

1 Pour prepared raspberry batter into prepared crust in springform pan.

2 Drop spoonfuls of chocolate batter over surface of raspberry batter.

3 Use knife or metal spatula and gently pull through both batters to create a marbled effect. Be careful not to over mix batters.

GRAND FINALE CHEESECAKE

1 SYMPHONY Milk Chocolate
  Bar or Milk Chocolate Bar
  With Almonds & Toffee Chips
  (7 oz.), broken into pieces
4 packages (3 oz. each) cream
  cheese, softened
½ cup sugar
2 tablespoons HERSHEY'S
  Cocoa
⅛ teaspoon salt
2 eggs
1 teaspoon vanilla extract
Almond Crust
Fresh fruit (blueberries, grapes,
  oranges, raspberries,
  strawberries)

Almond Crust
¾ cup graham cracker crumbs
⅔ cup chopped slivered almonds
2 tablespoons sugar
¼ cup (½ stick) butter or
  margarine, melted

▼ Heat oven to 325°F. In small microwave-safe bowl,
place chocolate. Microwave at HIGH (100%)
1 minute or until chocolate is melted and smooth
when stirred.

▼ In large mixer bowl, beat cream cheese until fluffy.
Stir together sugar, cocoa and salt; blend into cream
cheese mixture.

▼ Add eggs and vanilla; blend well. Add melted chocolate; beat just until blended. Pour into prepared
Almond Crust.

▼ Bake 35 to 40 minutes or until almost set. Remove
from oven to wire rack. With knife, loosen cake from
side of pan. Cool completely; remove side of pan.

▼ Refrigerate. Just before serving, garnish with fruit, if
desired. Cover; refrigerate leftover cheesecake.
8 servings.

▼ ALMOND CRUST: In medium bowl, stir together
graham cracker crumbs, almonds and sugar. Stir in
butter; blend well. Press mixture onto bottom and up
side of 8-inch springform pan or round pan with
removable bottom.

FUDGE TRUFFLE CHEESECAKE

2 cups (12-oz. pkg.)
  HERSHEY'S Semi-Sweet
  Chocolate Chips
3 packages (8 oz. each) cream
  cheese, softened
1 can (14 oz.) sweetened
  condensed milk
4 eggs
2 teaspoons vanilla extract
Chocolate Crumb Crust

▼ Heat oven to 300°F. In microwave-safe bowl,
place chocolate chips. Microwave at HIGH (100%)
1½ minutes; stir. If necessary, microwave at HIGH
additional 15 seconds at a time, stirring after each
heating, just until chips are melted and smooth
when stirred.

▼ In large mixer bowl, beat cream cheese until fluffy.
Gradually beat in sweetened condensed milk until
smooth. Add melted chocolate, eggs and vanilla; mix
well. Pour into prepared Chocolate Crumb Crust.
(continued)

Chocolate Crumb Crust
1½ cups vanilla wafer crumbs
½ cup powdered sugar
⅓ HERSHEY'S Cocoa
**⅓ cup butter or margarine,
  melted**

▼ Bake 1 hour and 5 minutes or until center is set. Remove from oven to wire rack. With knife, loosen cake from side of pan. Cool completely; remove side of pan. Refrigerate before serving. Garnish with coated chocolate truffles, if desired. Cover; refrigerate leftover cheesecake.
10 to 12 servings.

▼ CHOCOLATE CRUMB CRUST: In medium bowl, stir together wafer crumbs, powdered sugar, cocoa and butter. Press firmly onto bottom of 9-inch springform pan.

Grand Finale Cheesecake, Fudge Truffle Cheesecake

NEAPOLITAN CHEESECAKE

Neapolitan Cheesecake

**1 package (10 oz.) frozen strawberries, thawed and drained
thoroughly**

**½ cup HERSHEY'S Semi-Sweet
Chocolate Chips**

**3 packages (8 oz. each) cream
cheese, softened**

1½ cups sugar

3 eggs

⅓ cup dairy sour cream

**3 tablespoons plus 1 teaspoon
all-purpose flour, divided**

▼ Heat oven to 400°F. In blender or food processor,
puree strawberries to yield ½ cup; set aside.

▼ In small microwave-safe bowl, place chocolate chips.
Microwave at HIGH (100%) 1½ minutes; stir. If
necessary, microwave at HIGH an additional 15 seconds at a time, stirring after each heating, just until
chips are melted when stirred; set aside.

▼ In large mixer bowl, beat cream cheese with sugar
until smooth and creamy. Add eggs, sour cream,
3 tablespoons flour, vanilla and salt; beat until smooth.
(continued)

½ **teaspoon vanilla extract**
¼ **teaspoon salt**
¼ **teaspoon red food color (optional)**
Chocolate Crumb Crust

Chocolate Crumb Crust
1½ cups (about 45 wafers) vanilla wafer crumbs
½ **cup powdered sugar**
¼ **cup HERSHEY'S Cocoa**
⅓ **cup butter or margarine, melted**

▼ In separate bowl, stir together 1⅓ cups batter and remaining 1 teaspoon flour with strawberries; add food color, if desired. Pour strawberry batter into prepared Chocolate Crumb Crust.

▼ Carefully spoon 2 cups vanilla batter over strawberry batter; smooth surface. Stir melted chocolate into remaining batter; carefully spoon over vanilla batter, smoothing surface.

▼ Bake 10 minutes. Reduce oven temperature to 350°F; continue baking 55 to 60 minutes or until center of cheesecake is almost set. Remove from oven to wire rack. Cool 30 minutes.

▼ With knife, loosen cake from side of pan. Cool to room temperature; remove side of pan. Refrigerate several hours or overnight. Cover; refrigerate leftover cheesecake.
10 to 12 servings.

▼ CHOCOLATE CRUMB CRUST: Heat oven to 350°F. In small bowl, stir together vanilla wafer crumbs, powdered sugar and cocoa; blend in butter. Press mixture onto bottom of 9-inch springform pan. Bake 8 minutes; set aside.

*N*O-BAKE CHOCOLATE CHEESECAKE

1½ cups HERSHEY'S Semi-Sweet Chocolate Chips
1 package (8 oz.) cream cheese, softened
1 package (3 oz.) cream cheese, softened
½ **cup sugar**
¼ **cup (½ stick) butter or margarine, softened**
2 cups frozen non-dairy whipped topping, thawed
1 packaged graham cracker crumb crust (6 oz.)

▼ In small microwave-safe bowl, place chocolate chips. Microwave at HIGH (100%) 1 to 1½ minutes or until chips are melted and mixture is smooth when stirred. Set aside to cool.

▼ In large mixer bowl, beat cream cheese, sugar and butter until creamy; on low speed of electric mixer, blend in melted chocolate.

▼ Fold in whipped topping until blended; spoon into crust. Refrigerate until firm. Cover; refrigerate leftover cheesecake. Garnish as desired.
About 8 servings.

CREAMY PEANUT BUTTER CHIP CHEESECAKE

1¼ cups graham cracker crumbs

⅓ cup butter or margarine, melted

⅓ cup HERSHEY'S Cocoa or HERSHEY'S European Style Cocoa

⅓ cup plus 1½ cups sugar, divided

3 packages (8 oz. each) cream cheese, softened

4 eggs

2 teaspoons vanilla extract

1⅔ cups (10-oz. pkg.) REESE'S Peanut Butter Chips

Chocolate Drizzle

Chocolate Drizzle

½ cup HERSHEY'S Semi-Sweet Chocolate Chips

1 tablespoon shortening (do not use butter, margarine or oil)

▼ Heat oven to 350°F. In small bowl, stir together graham cracker crumbs, butter, cocoa and ⅓ cup sugar; press evenly onto bottom of 9-inch springform pan.

▼ In large mixer bowl, beat cream cheese and remaining 1½ cups sugar until smooth. Add eggs and vanilla; beat just until combined. Stir in peanut butter chips; pour over prepared crust.

▼ Bake 50 to 55 minutes or until slightly puffed and center is set except for 4-inch circle in center; remove from oven. Cool 30 minutes. With knife, loosen cheesecake from side of pan. Cool completely; remove side of pan.

▼ Using tip of spoon, drizzle Chocolate Drizzle across top of cheesecake. Refrigerate several hours before serving. Cover; refrigerate leftover cheesecake. *10 to 12 servings.*

▼ CHOCOLATE DRIZZLE: In small microwave-safe bowl, place chocolate chips and shortening. Microwave at HIGH (100%) 30 to 45 seconds or until chocolate is melted and mixture is smooth when stirred.

Creamy Peanut Butter Chip Cheesecake

CHOCOLATE PRALINE CHEESECAKE

1 cup pecan halves
3 tablespoons butter or
margarine
2 packages (8 oz. each) cream
cheese, softened
1 cup packed light brown sugar
⅓ cup HERSHEY'S Cocoa
3 eggs
1 teaspoon vanilla extract
Chocolate Crust
Sweetened whipped cream

Chocolate Crust
1 cup (about 30 wafers) vanilla
wafer crumbs
¼ cup HERSHEY'S Cocoa
¼ cup powdered sugar
¼ cup (½ stick) butter or
margarine, melted

▼ Set aside 12 pecan halves for garnish; finely chop remaining pecans to yield about ¾ cup.

▼ In medium skillet, melt butter; add chopped pecans. Cook over medium heat, stirring frequently, just until golden. Spoon pecans onto paper towels to drain.

▼ Heat oven to 400°F. In large mixer bowl, beat cream cheese and brown sugar until well blended. Add cocoa; beat until blended. Add eggs and vanilla; mix well. Stir in chopped pecans. Pour into prepared Chocolate Crust.

▼ Bake 10 minutes. Reduce oven temperature to 250°F; continue baking 45 minutes. With knife, loosen cake from side of pan. Cool completely; remove side of pan.

▼ Refrigerate at least 6 hours. Garnish with whipped cream and reserved pecan halves. Cover; refrigerate leftover cheesecake.
10 to 12 servings.

▼ CHOCOLATE CRUST: Heat oven to 350°F. In medium bowl, stir together vanilla wafer crumbs, cocoa and powdered sugar. Add butter; blend well. Press mixture onto bottom and 1 inch up side of 9-inch springform pan. Bake 8 minutes. Cool slightly.

CHOCOLATE CHIP PUMPKIN CHEESECAKE

1 cup (about 30 wafers) vanilla
    wafer crumbs
¼ cup HERSHEY'S Cocoa
¼ cup powdered sugar
¼ cup (½ stick) butter or
    margarine, melted
3 packages (8 oz. each) cream
    cheese, softened
1 cup granulated sugar
3 tablespoons all-purpose flour
1 teaspoon pumpkin pie spice
1 cup canned pumpkin
4 eggs
1½ cups HERSHEY'S MINI
    CHIPS Semi-Sweet Chocolate
Chocolate Leaves (optional, see
    page 181)

▼ Heat oven to 350°F. In medium bowl, stir together crumbs, cocoa and powdered sugar; stir in butter. Press mixture onto bottom and ½ inch up side of 9-inch springform pan. Bake 8 minutes. Remove from oven; cool slightly. Increase oven temperature to 400°F.

▼ In large mixer bowl, beat cream cheese, granulated sugar, flour and pumpkin pie spice until well blended. Add pumpkin and eggs; beat until well blended. Stir in small chocolate chips; pour batter into prepared crust.

▼ Bake 10 minutes. Reduce oven temperature to 250°F; continue baking 50 minutes. Remove from oven to wire rack. With knife, loosen cake from side of pan.

▼ Cool completely; remove side of pan. Refrigerate before serving. Garnish with Chocolate Leaves, if desired. Cover; refrigerate leftover cheesecake. *10 to 12 servings.*

Chocolate Chip Pumpkin Cheesecake

HERSHEY BAR CHEESECAKE

1 HERSHEY'S Milk Chocolate
Bar (7 oz.), broken into pieces
4 packages (3 oz. each) cream
cheese, softened
¾ cup sugar
2 tablespoons HERSHEY'S
Cocoa
Dash salt
2 eggs
½ teaspoon vanilla extract
Almond Crust
Sour Cream Topping

Almond Crust
¾ cup graham cracker crumbs
⅔ cup chopped slivered almonds
2 tablespoons sugar
¼ cup (½ stick) butter or
margarine, melted

Sour Cream Topping
½ cup dairy sour cream
2 tablespoons sugar
½ teaspoon vanilla extract

▼ Heat oven to 325°F. In top of double boiler over hot, not boiling, water, melt chocolate bar pieces; set aside.

▼ In large mixer bowl, beat cream cheese until light and fluffy. Stir together sugar, cocoa and salt; blend into cream cheese mixture. Beat in eggs and vanilla. Add reserved melted chocolate; beat just until blended (do not overbeat). Pour batter into Almond Crust.

▼ Bake 35 to 40 minutes or until set. Remove from oven to wire rack. With knife, loosen cake from side of pan; cool to room temperature.

▼ Spread Sour Cream Topping over cheesecake. Refrigerate several hours or overnight; remove side of pan. Cover; refrigerate leftover cheesecake. *8 servings.*

▼ ALMOND CRUST: In medium bowl, stir together graham cracker crumbs, almonds and sugar. Stir in butter; blend well. Press mixture onto bottom and up side of 8-inch springform pan or round pan with removable bottom.

▼ SOUR CREAM TOPPING: In small bowl, stir together sour cream, sugar and vanilla.

CHEWY CHOCOLATE OATMEAL COOKIES

½ cup (1 stick) butter or
   margarine, melted
½ cup HERSHEY'S Cocoa
1 can (14 oz.) sweetened
   condensed milk
2 eggs, beaten
2 teaspoons vanilla extract
1½ cups quick-cooking
   rolled oats
1 cup all-purpose biscuit
   baking mix
¼ teaspoon salt
1⅔ cups (10-oz. pkg.)
   HERSHEY'S Vanilla Milk
   Chips
1⅔ cups (10-oz. pkg.) REESE'S
   Peanut Butter Chips

▼ Heat oven to 350°F. Lightly grease cookie sheet. In
large bowl, stir together butter and cocoa until mixture is smooth.

▼ Stir in sweetened condensed milk, eggs, vanilla
extract, oats, baking mix, salt, vanilla milk chips and
peanut butter chips until well blended. Let batter rest
10 minutes; drop by heaping teaspoonfuls onto
prepared cookie sheet.

▼ Bake 7 to 9 minutes or until tops begin to dry
(do not overbake). Cool 5 minutes; remove from
cookie sheet to wire rack. Cool completely. Store in
airtight container.
About 4 dozen cookies.

HERSHEY'S MORE CHIPS CHOCOLATE CHIP COOKIES

1½ cups (3 sticks) butter,
   softened
1 cup granulated sugar
1 cup packed light brown sugar
3 eggs
2 teaspoons vanilla extract
3⅓ cups all-purpose flour
1½ teaspoons baking soda
¾ teaspoon salt
4 cups (24-oz. pkg.) HERSHEY'S
   Semi-Sweet Chocolate Chips

▼ Heat oven to 375°F. In large mixer bowl, beat butter,
granulated sugar and brown sugar until creamy. Add
eggs and vanilla; beat until light and fluffy.

▼ Stir together flour, baking soda and salt; gradually
beat into butter mixture. Stir in chocolate chips.
Drop by rounded teaspoonfuls onto ungreased
cookie sheet.

▼ Bake 8 to 10 minutes or until lightly browned.
Cool slightly; remove from cookie sheet to wire rack.
Cool completely.
About 7½ dozen cookies.

Chewy Chocolate Oatmeal Cookies, Hershey's More Chips Chocolate Chip Cookies

$\mathcal{S}$ECRET KISS COOKIES

1 cup (2 sticks) butter or margarine, softened
½ cup granulated sugar
1 teaspoon vanilla extract
1¾ cups all-purpose flour
1 cup finely chopped walnuts
1 bag (6 oz.) HERSHEY'S KISSES Milk Chocolates
Powdered sugar

▼ In large mixer bowl, beat butter, granulated sugar and vanilla until light and fluffy. Add flour and walnuts; beat on low speed of electric mixer until well blended. Cover; refrigerate dough 1 to 2 hours or until firm enough to handle.

▼ Remove wrappers from chocolate pieces. Heat oven to 375°F. Using approximately 1 tablespoon of dough for each cookie, shape dough around each chocolate piece; roll to make ball. (Be sure to cover each chocolate piece completely.) Place on ungreased cookie sheet.

▼ Bake 10 to 12 minutes or until cookies are set but not brown. Cool slightly; remove from cookie sheet to wire rack.

▼ While still slightly warm, roll in powdered sugar. Cool completely. Store in tightly covered container. Roll again in powdered sugar just before serving. *About 3 dozen cookies.*

Note: For variety, sift together 1 tablespoon HERSHEY'S Cocoa with ⅓ cup powdered sugar. Roll warm cookies in cocoa mixture.

1 Wrap cookie dough around each unwrapped HERSHEY'S KISSES Milk Chocolate.

2 After baking, roll cookies are in powdered sugar.

3 Finished cookies ready for serving.

℘EANUT BUTTER COOKIES

¼ **cup (½ stick) butter or margarine, softened**
¼ **cup shortening**
½ **cup REESE'S Creamy Peanut Butter**
½ **cup granulated sugar**
½ **cup packed light brown sugar**
1 **egg**
1¼ **cups all-purpose flour**
¾ **teaspoon baking soda**
½ **teaspoon baking powder**
¼ **teaspoon salt**
¾ **cup REESE'S Peanut Butter Chips**

▼ Heat oven to 375°F. In large mixer bowl, beat butter, shortening, peanut butter, granulated sugar, brown sugar and egg.

▼ Stir together flour, baking soda, baking powder and salt; add to butter mixture, beating until well blended. Stir in peanut butter chips.

▼ Shape into 1-inch balls; place on ungreased cookie sheet. With fork dipped in sugar, flatten in criss-cross pattern.

▼ Bake 10 to 12 minutes or until set. Cool slightly; remove from cookie sheet to wire rack. Cool completely.
About 4 dozen cookies.

Peanut Butter Cookies, Secret Kiss Cookiess

HERSHEY'S BEST BROWNIES

1 cup (2 sticks) butter or
  margarine
2 cups sugar
2 teaspoons vanilla extract
4 eggs
¾ cup HERSHEY'S Cocoa or
  HERSHEY'S European Style
  Cocoa
1 cup all-purpose flour
½ teaspoon baking powder
¼ teaspoon salt
1 cup chopped nuts (optional)

▼ Heat oven to 350°F. Grease 13 x 9 x 2-inch baking pan. In large microwave-safe bowl, place butter. Microwave at HIGH (100%) 2 to 2½ minutes or until melted.

▼ Stir in sugar and vanilla. Add eggs, one at a time, beating well with spoon after each addition.

▼ Add cocoa; beat until well blended. Add flour, baking powder and salt; beat well. Stir in nuts, if desired. Pour batter into prepared pan.

▼ Bake 30 to 35 minutes or until brownies begin to pull away from sides of pan. Cool completely in pan on wire rack. Cut into bars.
About 36 brownies.

Marbled Cherry Brownies, Hershey's Best Brownies

Marbled Cherry Brownies

½ cup (1 stick) butter or
    margarine, melted
⅓ cup HERSHEY'S Cocoa
2 eggs
1 cup sugar
1 teaspoon vanilla extract
½ cup all-purpose flour
½ teaspoon baking powder
¼ teaspoon salt
Cherry Cream Filling

Cherry Cream Filling
1 package (3 oz.) cream cheese,
    softened
¼ cup sugar
1 egg
½ teaspoon vanilla extract
¼ teaspoon almond extract
⅓ cup chopped maraschino
    cherries, well drained
1 to 2 drops red food color
    (optional)

▼ Heat oven to 350°F. Grease 9-inch square baking pan. In small bowl, stir butter and cocoa until well blended; cool slightly. In small mixer bowl, beat eggs until foamy. Gradually add sugar and vanilla, beating until well blended.

▼ Stir together flour, baking powder and salt; add to egg mixture. Add cocoa mixture; stir until well blended. Spread half of chocolate batter into prepared pan; cover with Cherry Cream Filling.

▼ Drop spoonfuls of remaining chocolate batter over filling. With knife or spatula, gently swirl chocolate batter into filling for marbled effect.

▼ Bake 35 to 40 minutes or until brownies begin to pull away from sides of pan. Cool; cut into squares. Cover; refrigerate leftover brownies. Bring to room temperature to serve.
About 16 brownies.

▼ CHERRY CREAM FILLING: In small mixer bowl, beat cream cheese and sugar until blended. Add egg, vanilla and almond extract; beat well. Stir in cherries and food color, if desired.

Tropical Gardens Cookies

½ cup (1 stick) butter or
    margarine, softened
½ cup shortening
1 cup granulated sugar
¼ cup packed light brown sugar
1 teaspoon vanilla extract
1 egg
1 tablespoon freshly grated
    orange peel
2¾ cups all-purpose flour
1½ teaspoons baking soda
1 teaspoon salt
¼ cup orange juice
2 cups (12-oz. pkg.) HERSHEY'S
    MINI CHIPS Semi-Sweet
    Chocolate
Granulated sugar

▼ In large mixer bowl, beat butter, shortening, 1 cup granulated sugar, brown sugar and vanilla until light and fluffy. Add egg and orange peel; blend well.

▼ Stir together flour, baking soda and salt; add alternately with orange juice to butter mixture. Stir in small chocolate chips. Cover; refrigerate dough about 1 hour or until firm enough to handle.

▼ Heat oven to 350°F. Shape dough into 1-inch balls; roll in granulated sugar. Place on ungreased cookie sheet; flatten by crisscrossing with tines of fork.

▼ Bake 8 to 10 minutes or until lightly browned. Cool slightly; remove from cookie sheet to wire rack. Cool completely.
About 7 dozen cookies.

CHOCOLATE PEANUT BUTTER THUMBPRINTS

1²⁄₃ cups (10-oz. pkg.) REESE'S Peanut Butter Chips, divided
½ cup (1 stick) butter or margarine, softened
½ cup granulated sugar
½ cup packed light brown sugar
1 egg
1 teaspoon vanilla extract
1½ cups all-purpose flour
½ cup HERSHEY'S Cocoa or HERSHEY'S European Style Cocoa
½ teaspoon baking soda
Additional granulated sugar

▼ Heat oven to 375°F. In small microwave-safe bowl, place ½ cup peanut butter chips. Microwave at HIGH (100%) 30 to 40 seconds or just until chips are melted and smooth when stirred; set aside.

▼ In large mixer bowl, beat butter, granulated sugar, brown sugar, egg and vanilla until light and fluffy. Add melted peanut butter chips; beat well.

▼ Stir together flour, cocoa and baking soda; stir into peanut butter mixture until well blended.

▼ For each cookie, shape 1 tablespoon dough into ball; roll in additional granulated sugar. Place balls on ungreased cookie sheet; with bottom of glass, flatten cookies to ¼-inch thickness. Using thumb, make indentation in center of each cookie.

▼ Bake 6 to 8 minutes or just until set. Remove from oven. If necessary, using tip of spoon, press indentation in center of each cookie; immediately place 1 teaspoonful peanut butter chips in each indentation. Soften 1 to 2 minutes; spread melted chips into swirl. Remove from cookie sheet to wire rack. Cool completely.
About 2 ½ dozen cookies.

1 Flatten unbaked cookies with bottom of glass.

2 Immediately after baking, place peanut butter chips in indentation to soften.

3 After chips have softened and melted, spread chips in swirl design with small spatula.

PEANUT BUTTER CHOCOLATE CHUNK BROWNIES

1⅔ cups (10-oz. pkg.) REESE'S
   Peanut Butter Chips
½ cup (1 stick) butter or
   margarine, softened
1 cup sugar
3 eggs
1 teaspoon vanilla extract
1 cup all-purpose flour
½ teaspoon salt
1¾ cups (10-oz. pkg.)
   HERSHEY'S Semi-Sweet
   Chocolate Chunks
¼ cup chopped peanuts

▼ Heat oven to 350°F. Grease 13 x 9 x 2-inch baking pan. In medium microwave-safe bowl, place peanut butter chips. Microwave at HIGH (100%) 1 minute; stir. If necessary, microwave at HIGH an additional 30 seconds or until chips are melted and smooth when stirred; cool slightly.

▼ Meanwhile, in large mixer bowl, beat butter and sugar until light and fluffy; add eggs and vanilla. Beat in melted peanut butter chips, flour and salt; stir in chocolate chunks and peanuts. Spread batter into prepared pan.

▼ Bake 30 to 35 minutes or until brownies begin to pull away from sides of pan. Cool completely in pan on wire rack. Cut into squares.
About 3 dozen brownies.

Chocolate Peanut Butter Thumbprints, Peanut Butter Chocolate Chunk Brownies

CHIPPY CHEWY BARS

½ cup (1 stick) butter or margarine

1½ cups graham cracker crumbs

1⅔ cups (10-oz. pkg.) REESE'S Peanut Butter Chips, divided

1½ cups flaked coconut

1 can (14 oz.) sweetened condensed milk

1 cup HERSHEY'S Semi-Sweet Chocolate Chips

1½ teaspoons shortening (do not use butter, margarine or oil)

▼ Heat oven to 350°F. Place butter in 13 x 9 x 2-inch baking pan. Heat in oven until melted; remove pan from oven.

▼ Sprinkle graham cracker crumbs evenly over butter; press down with fork. Layer 1 cup peanut butter chips over crumbs; sprinkle coconut over peanut butter chips. Layer remaining ⅔ cup peanut butter chips over coconut; drizzle sweetened condensed milk evenly over top.

▼ Bake 20 minutes or until lightly browned. Remove from oven.

▼ In small microwave-safe bowl, place chocolate chips and shortening. Microwave at HIGH (100%) 1 minute; stir. If necessary, microwave at HIGH an additional 15 seconds at a time, stirring after each heating, just until chips are melted and mixture is smooth. Drizzle evenly over top of baked mixture. Cool completely in pan on wire rack. Cut into bars. *About 48 bars.*

Chippy Chewy Bars

CHOCOLATE CRINKLE COOKIES

2 cups granulated sugar
¾ cup vegetable oil
¾ cup HERSHEY'S Cocoa
4 eggs
2 teaspoons vanilla extract
2⅓ cups all-purpose flour
2 teaspoons baking powder
½ teaspoon salt
Powdered sugar

▼ In large mixer bowl, stir together granulated sugar and oil; add cocoa, blending well. Beat in eggs and vanilla.

▼ Stir together flour, baking powder and salt; add to cocoa mixture, blending well. Cover; refrigerate until dough is firm enough to handle, at least 6 hours.

▼ Heat oven to 350°F. Grease cookie sheet. Shape dough into 1-inch balls; roll in powdered sugar. Place about 2 inches apart on prepared cookie sheet.

▼ Bake 12 to 14 minutes or until almost no indentation remains when touched lightly and tops are crackled. Remove from cookie sheet to wire rack. Cool completely.
About 4 dozen cookies.

Chocolate Crinkle Cookies

CHOCOLATE SPRITZ COOKIES

1 cup (2 sticks) butter, softened
⅔ cup sugar
1 egg
1 teaspoon vanilla extract
2¼ cups all-purpose flour
⅓ cup HERSHEY'S Cocoa
½ teaspoon salt
Colored sprinkles (optional)
Chopped maraschino cherries
  (optional)

▼ Heat oven to 350°F. In large mixer bowl, beat butter, sugar, egg and vanilla until light and fluffy. Stir together flour, cocoa and salt; gradually add to butter mixture, beating until well blended.

▼ Fill cookie press with dough. Press dough onto cool, ungreased cookie sheet. Garnish with sprinkles or cherries, if desired.

▼ Bake 5 to 7 minutes or just until set. Remove from cookie sheet to wire rack. Cool completely.
About 4 ½ dozen cookies.

▼ **Variation**
CHOCOLATE DIPPED SPRITZ COOKIES
Prepare dough as directed above. Press dough onto cool, ungreased cookie sheet with ribbon plate in cookie press. Bake and cool as directed. Melt 1 cup HERSHEY'S Semi-Sweet Chocolate Chips with 1 tablespoon shortening (do not use butter, margarine or oil). Gently dip part of each cookie into chocolate. Place on wax paper-covered tray. Refrigerate until firm.

QUICK & CHEWY CHOCOLATE DROPS

1 package (8 oz.) HERSHEY'S
Semi-Sweet Baking Chocolate,
broken into pieces
¼ cup (½ stick) butter or
margarine, softened
½ cup sugar
1 egg
1½ teaspoons vanilla extract
½ cup all-purpose flour
¼ teaspoon baking powder
½ cup chopped nuts (optional)

▼ Heat oven to 350°F. In small microwave-safe bowl, place chocolate. Microwave at HIGH (100%) 1½ to 2 minutes or until chocolate is melted when stirred; cool slightly.

▼ In large mixer bowl, beat butter and sugar until well blended. Add egg and vanilla; beat well.

▼ Blend in melted chocolate, flour and baking powder. Stir in nuts, if desired. Drop by rounded teaspoonfuls onto ungreased cookie sheet.

▼ Bake 8 to 10 minutes or until almost set. Cool slightly; remove from cookie sheet to wire rack. Cool completely. Garnish as desired.
About 2 dozen cookies.

PEANUT BUTTER CUP COOKIES

About 40 (14-oz. pkg.) REESE'S
  Peanut Butter Cups Miniatures
½ cup (1 stick) butter or
  margarine, softened
½ cup REESE'S Creamy Peanut
  Butter
½ cup packed light brown sugar
¼ cup granulated sugar
1 egg
1⅔ cups all-purpose flour
1 teaspoon baking soda
1 egg white
1 tablespoon water
1 cup crushed corn flakes

▼ Heat oven to 375°F. Remove wrappers from peanut butter cups. In large mixer bowl, beat butter, peanut butter, brown sugar and granulated sugar until light and fluffy; blend in egg.

▼ Stir together flour and baking soda; add to butter mixture.

▼ Shape dough into 1-inch balls. Stir together egg white and water; beat with fork until foamy. Roll balls in egg white mixture, then in crushed cereal. Place on ungreased cookie sheet; press with thumb or finger tips in center making an indentation.

▼ Bake 8 to 10 minutes or until cookies are set. Remove from oven; and immediately press peanut butter cup onto each cookie. Cool 1 minute; remove carefully from cookie sheet to wire rack. Cool completely. *About 3½ dozen cookies.*

Quick & Chewy Chocolate Drops, Peanut Butter Cup Cookies, Chocolate Spritz Cookies

S'MORES

4 graham crackers
1 HERSHEY'S Milk Chocolate Bar (1.55 oz.)
4 large marshmallows

▼ Break graham crackers in half. Break chocolate bar into 4 sections. Center one section on each of 4 graham cracker halves. Top each with marshmallow.

▼ Place on paper towel. Microwave at HIGH (100%) 10 to 15 seconds or until marshmallow puffs. Top each with another graham cracker half; press gently. Let stand 1 minute to soften chocolate. Serve immediately. *4 snacks.*

▼ CONVENTIONAL METHOD: Center chocolate section on each of 4 graham cracker halves; set aside. Place remaining graham cracker halves on cookie sheet. Top each with marshmallow. On middle oven rack, broil several minutes or just until marshmallows are golden brown. Immediately invert onto chocolate-topped graham crackers; press gently. Let stand 1 minute to soften chocolate. Serve immediately.

▼ **Variation**
PEANUTTY S'MORES
Spread thin layer of peanut butter on graham cracker or substitute 1.85-ounce MR. GOODBAR for milk chocolate bar. Proceed as directed.

S'MORE CEREAL SQUARES

½ cup light corn syrup
4 HERSHEY'S Milk Chocolate Bars (1.55 oz. each), broken into pieces
½ teaspoon vanilla extract
3½ cups honey graham cereal
1 cup miniature marshmallows

▼ Butter 8-inch square pan. In 3-quart saucepan over medium heat, cook corn syrup to boiling or place in large microwave-safe bowl and microwave at HIGH (100%) 1 minute or to boiling. Remove from heat or microwave oven; add chocolate and vanilla, stir until chocolate is melted.

▼ Gradually fold in cereal until coated with chocolate. Fold in marshmallows. Press mixture into prepared pan; refrigerate until firm, about 30 minutes. Cut into bars. Refrigerate leftover bars to retain crispness. *24 bars.*

S'MORE COOKIE BARS

½ cup (1 stick) butter or margarine, softened
¾ cup sugar
1 egg
1 teaspoon vanilla extract
1⅓ cups all-purpose flour
¾ cup graham cracker crumbs
1 teaspoon baking powder
¼ teaspoon salt
4 HERSHEY'S Milk Chocolate Bars (1.55 oz. each)
1 cup marshmallow creme

▼ Heat oven to 350°F. Grease 8-inch square baking pan. In large mixer bowl, beat butter and sugar until light and fluffy. Add egg and vanilla; beat well.

▼ Stir together flour, graham cracker crumbs, baking powder and salt; add to butter mixture, beating until blended.

▼ Press half of dough into prepared pan. Arrange chocolate bars over dough, breaking as needed to fit. Spread with marshmallow creme. Scatter bits of remaining dough over marshmallow; carefully press to form a layer.

▼ Bake 30 to 35 minutes or until lightly browned. Cool completely in pan on wire rack. Cut into bars. *16 bars.*

S'mores, S'more Cereal Squares, S'more Cookie Bars

DEEP DARK CHOCOLATE COOKIES

¾ cup (1½ sticks) butter or margarine, softened
¾ cup granulated sugar
½ cup packed light brown sugar
1 teaspoon vanilla extract
2 eggs
1¾ cups all-purpose flour
½ cup HERSHEY'S Cocoa
¾ teaspoon baking soda
½ teaspoon baking powder
¼ teaspoon salt
1 cup HERSHEY'S Semi-Sweet Chocolate Chips
½ cup chopped nuts

▼ Heat oven to 375°F. In large mixer bowl, beat butter, granulated sugar, brown sugar and vanilla with an electric mixer on medium speed about 2 minutes or until well blended. Add eggs; beat well.

▼ Stir together flour, cocoa, baking soda, baking powder and salt; gradually add to butter mixture, beating just until blended. Stir in chocolate chips and nuts. Drop by heaping teaspoonfuls onto cookie sheet.

▼ Bake 7 minutes or until set. Cool 1 minute; remove from cookie sheet to wire rack. Cool completely.
About 4 dozen cookies.

CHOCOLATE THUMBPRINT COOKIES

½ cup (1 stick) butter or margarine, softened
⅔ cup sugar
1 egg, separated
2 tablespoons milk
1 teaspoon vanilla extract
1 cup all-purpose flour
⅓ cup HERSHEY'S Cocoa
¼ teaspoon salt
1 cup chopped nuts
Vanilla Filling
26 HERSHEY'S KISSES Milk Chocolates, pecan halves or candied cherry halves

Vanilla Filling
½ cup powdered sugar
1 tablespoon butter or margarine, softened
2 teaspoons milk
¼ teaspoon vanilla extract

▼ In small mixer bowl, beat butter, sugar, egg yolk, milk and vanilla until light and fluffy. Stir together flour, cocoa and salt; gradually add to butter mixture, beating until blended. Refrigerate dough until firm enough to handle.

▼ Heat oven to 350°F. Lightly grease cookie sheet. Shape dough into 1-inch balls. Beat egg white slightly. Dip each ball into egg white; roll in nuts. Place on prepared cookie sheet. Press thumb gently in center of each cookie.

▼ Bake 10 to 12 minutes or until set. Meanwhile, remove wrappers from chocolate pieces.

▼ As soon as cookies are removed from oven, spoon about ¼ teaspoon Vanilla Filling into thumbprint. Gently press chocolate piece in center of each cookie. Remove carefully from cookie sheet to wire rack. Cool completely.
About 2 dozen cookies.

▼ VANILLA FILLING: In small bowl, beat powdered sugar, butter, milk and vanilla until smooth.

COCOA CHERRY DROPS

½ cup (1 stick) plus 2 tablespoons butter or margarine, softened
1 cup sugar
1 egg
1 teaspoon vanilla extract
1¼ cups all-purpose flour
6 tablespoons HERSHEY'S Cocoa
½ teaspoon baking soda
½ teaspoon salt
1 cup maraschino cherries, well-drained
½ cup chopped walnuts
Walnut pieces (optional)

▼ Heat oven to 350°F. In large mixer bowl, beat butter and sugar until light and fluffy; beat in egg and vanilla.

▼ Stir together flour, cocoa, baking soda and salt; stir into butter mixture. Stir in cherries and walnuts. Drop by rounded teaspoonfuls onto ungreased cookie sheet. Press nut piece onto each cookie, if desired.

▼ Bake 10 to 12 minutes or until set. Cool slightly; remove from cookie sheet to wire rack. Cool completely.
About 4 dozen cookies.

Chocolate Thumbprint Cookies, Cocoa Cherry Drops

QUICK & EASY FUDGEY BROWNIES

4 bars (4 oz.) HERSHEY'S Unsweetened Baking Chocolate, broken into pieces
¾ cup (1½ sticks) butter or margarine
2 cups sugar
3 eggs
1½ teaspoons vanilla extract
1 cup all-purpose flour
1 cup chopped nuts (optional)
Quick & Easy Chocolate Frosting (optional)

Quick & Easy Chocolate Frosting
3 bars (3 oz.) HERSHEY'S Unsweetened Baking Chocolate, broken into pieces
1 cup miniature marshmallows
½ cup (1 stick) butter or margarine, softened
⅓ cup milk
2½ cups powdered sugar
½ teaspoon vanilla extract

▼ Heat oven to 350°F. Grease 13 x 9 x 2-inch baking pan. In large microwave-safe bowl, place chocolate and butter. Microwave at HIGH (100%) 1½ to 2 minutes or until chocolate is melted and mixture is smooth when stirred.

▼ Add sugar; stir with spoon until well blended. Add eggs and vanilla; mix well. Add flour and nuts, if desired; stir until well blended. Spread into prepared pan.

▼ Bake 30 to 35 minutes or until wooden pick inserted in center comes out almost clean. Cool in pan on wire rack. Frost with Quick & Easy Chocolate Frosting, if desired. Cut into squares.
About 24 brownies

▼ QUICK & EASY CHOCOLATE FROSTING: In medium saucepan over low heat, melt chocolate, stirring constantly. Add marshmallows; stir frequently until melted. (Mixture will be very thick and will pull away from sides of pan.) Spoon mixture into small mixer bowl; beat in butter. Add milk gradually, beating until smooth. Add powdered sugar and vanilla; beat to desired consistency.
About 2 ¼ cups frosting.

CHOCOLATE CHUNK BUTTER PECAN BARS

1 cup (2 sticks) butter or margarine, softened
1 cup packed light brown sugar
1 egg yolk
1 teaspoon vanilla extract
2 cups all-purpose flour
¼ teaspoon salt
1¾ cups (10-oz. pkg.) HERSHEY'S Semi-Sweet Chocolate Chunks
½ to 1 cup coarsely chopped pecans

▼ Heat oven to 350°F. Grease 13 x 9 x 2-inch baking pan. In large mixer bowl, stir together butter, brown sugar, egg yolk and vanilla; blend in flour and salt. Press mixture onto bottom of prepared pan.

▼ Bake 25 to 30 minutes or until lightly browned.

▼ Remove from oven; immediately sprinkle chocolate chunks on crust. Let stand until softened, about 5 minutes; spread evenly over crust. Sprinkle pecans over top. Cool completely in pan on wire rack. Cut into bars.
About 36 bars.

Chocolate Chunk Butter Pecan Bars, Quick & Easy Fudgey Brownies

REESE'S PIECES CHOCOLATE COOKIES

½ cup (1 stick) butter or margarine
1 cup sugar
1 egg
1 teaspoon vanilla extract
1½ cups all-purpose flour
⅓ cup HERSHEY'S Cocoa
½ teaspoon baking soda
½ teaspoon salt
¼ cup milk
1¼ cups REESE'S PIECES Candy, divided

▼ Heat oven to 375°F. In large mixer bowl, beat butter, sugar, egg and vanilla until well blended. Stir together flour, cocoa, baking soda and salt; add alternately with milk to butter mixture, beating until well blended.

▼ Stir in ¾ cup candies. Drop by teaspoonful onto ungreased cookie sheet. Place 2 or 3 of remaining candies on top of each cookie near center.

▼ Bake 10 to 11 minutes or until soft-set (do not over-bake). Cool 1 minute; remove from cookie sheet to wire rack. Cool completely.
About 3½ dozen cookies.

REESE'S PIECES ICE CREAM SAUCERS

½ cup shortening
1 cup sugar
1 egg
1 teaspoon vanilla extract
1½ cups plus 2 tablespoons all-purpose flour
⅓ cup HERSHEY'S Cocoa
½ teaspoon baking soda
½ teaspoon salt
¼ cup milk
1¼ cups REESE'S PIECES Candy, divided
Vanilla ice cream

▼ Follow directions above to prepare recipe except use shortening in place of butter and do not add candies to batter. Refrigerate batter about 1 hour.

▼ Drop by heaping tablepoonfuls about 2 inches apart onto ungreased cookie sheet. Flatten each with palm of hand or bottom of glass into 2¼-inch circle about ¼-inch thick; evenly space 8 to 10 candies on top of each.

▼ Bake at 375°F for 8 to 10 minutes or until almost set. Cool 1 minute; remove from cookie sheet to wire rack. Cool completely.

▼ Place scoop slightly softened ice cream on flat side of one cookie; spread evenly with spatula. Top with second cookie, pressing lightly. Wrap in plastic wrap; immediately place in freezer. Freeze until firm.
About twelve 4-inch ice cream sandwiches.

REESE'S PIECES OATMEAL BARS

⅔ cup shortening
½ cup packed light brown sugar
⅓ cup granulated sugar
1 egg
1 teaspoon vanilla extract
1 cup all-purpose flour
½ teaspoon baking soda
½ teaspoon salt
¼ cup milk
1½ cups regular or quick-
   cooking oats
1½ cups REESE'S PIECES
   Candy, divided

▼ Heat oven to 350°F. Grease 13 x 9 x 2-inch baking pan. In large mixer bowl, beat shortening, brown sugar and granulated sugar until light and fluffy. Add egg and vanilla; beat well.

▼ Stir together flour, baking soda and salt; add alternately with milk to shortening mixture. Stir in oats and 1 cup candies. Spread batter into prepared pan. Sprinkle remaining candies on top.

▼ Bake 25 to 30 minutes or until edges are firm and golden brown. Cool completely in pan on wire rack. Cut into bars
About 36 bars.

▼ **Variation:**
Prepare batter as directed above, except drop batter onto ungreased cookie sheet. Place 3 or 4 candies near center of each cookie. Bake at 350°F 12 minutes or until edges are lightly browned. Cool 1 minute; remove from cookie sheet to wire rack. Cool completely.
About 4 dozen cookies.

Reese's Pieces Oatmeal Bars, Reese's Pieces Chocolate Cookies, Reese's Pieces Ice Cream Saucers

ᵖEANUT BLOSSOMS

1 bag (9 oz.) HERSHEY'S KISSES Milk Chocolates
½ cup shortening
¾ cup REESE'S Creamy or Crunchy Peanut Butter
⅓ cup granulated sugar
⅓ cup packed light brown sugar
1 egg
2 tablespoons milk
1 teaspoon vanilla extract
1½ cups all-purpose flour
1 teaspoon baking soda
½ teaspoon salt
Granulated sugar

▼ Heat oven to 375°F. Remove wrappers from chocolate pieces. In large mixer bowl, beat shortening and peanut butter until well blended.

▼ Add ⅓ cup granulated sugar and brown sugar; beat until light and fluffy. Add egg, milk and vanilla; beat well.

▼ Stir together flour, baking soda and salt; gradually add to peanut butter mixture. Shape dough into 1-inch balls. Roll in granulated sugar; place on ungreased cookie sheet.

▼ Bake 10 to 12 minutes or until lightly browned. Immediately place chocolate piece on top of each cookie, pressing down so cookie cracks around edges. Remove from cookie sheet to wire rack. Cool completely.
About 4 dozen cookies.

1 Roll prepared cookie dough between the hand to form balls.

2 Roll each ball in sugar and place on cookie sheet.

3 After baking, place HERSHEY'S KISSES Milk Chocolate on each cookie.

VANILLA CHIP APRICOT OATMEAL COOKIES

¾ cup (1½ sticks) butter or
  margarine, softened
½ cup granulated sugar
½ cup packed light brown sugar
1 egg
1 cup all-purpose flour
1 teaspoon baking soda
2½ cups rolled oats
1⅔ cups (10-oz. pkg.)
  HERSHEY'S Vanilla Milk
  Chips
½ cup chopped dried apricots

▼ Heat oven to 375°F. In large mixer bowl, beat butter, granulated sugar and brown sugar until light and fluffy. Add egg; beat well. Add flour and baking soda; beat until well blended. Stir in oats, vanilla milk chips and dried apricots. Drop by rounded teaspoonfuls onto ungreased cookie sheet.

▼ Bake 8 to 10 minutes or just until lightly browned; do not overbake. Cool slightly; remove from cookie sheet to wire rack. Cool completely.
About 3½ dozen cookies.

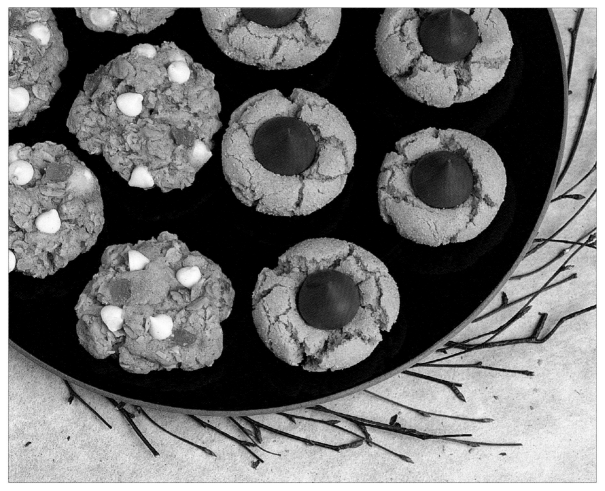

Vanilla Chip Apricot Oatmeal Cookies, Peanut Blossoms

PEANUT BUTTER CUT-OUT COOKIES

½ cup (1 stick) butter or
  margarine
1 cup REESE'S Peanut Butter
  Chips
⅔ cup packed light brown
  sugar
1 egg
¾ teaspoon vanilla extract
1⅓ cups all-purpose flour
¾ teaspoon baking soda
½ cup finely chopped pecans
Chocolate Chip Glaze or Peanut
  Butter Chip Glaze

Chocolate Chip Glaze
1 cup HERSHEY'S Semi-Sweet
  Chocolate Chips
1 tablespoon shortening (do not
  use butter, margarine or oil)

Peanut Butter Chip Glaze
⅔ cup REESE'S Peanut Butter
  Chips
1 tablespoon shortening (do not
  use butter, margarine or oil)

▼ In medium saucepan, combine butter and peanut butter chips; cook over low heat, stirring constantly, until melted. Pour into large mixer bowl; add brown sugar, egg and vanilla, beating until well blended. Stir in flour, baking soda and pecans; blend well. Refrigerate 15 to 20 minutes or until firm enough to roll.

▼ Heat oven to 350°F. Roll out dough, a small portion at a time, on lightly floured board or between 2 pieces of wax paper to ¼-inch thickness. (Keep remaining dough in refrigerator.) With cookie cutters, cut into desired shapes; place on ungreased cookie sheet.

▼ Bake 7 to 8 minutes or until almost set (do not overbake). Cool 1 minute; remove from cookie sheet to wire rack. Cool completely.

▼ Drizzle Chocolate Chip Glaze or Peanut Butter Chip Glaze onto each cookie; garnish as desired.
About 3 dozen cookies.

▼ CHOCOLATE CHIP GLAZE: In small microwave-safe bowl, place chocolate chips and shortening. Microwave at HIGH (100%) 1 minute; stir. If necessary, microwave at HIGH an additional 15 seconds at a time, stirring after each heating, just until chips are melted when stirred.
About ½ cup glaze.

▼ PEANUT BUTTER CHIP GLAZE: In small microwave-safe bowl, place peanut butter chips and shortening. Microwave at HIGH (100%) 30 seconds; stir. Microwave at HIGH an additional 30 seconds, stir until smooth.
About ⅓ cup glaze.

▼ **Variation**
SLICE & BAKE PEANUT BUTTER COOKIES
Prepare dough as directed above. Refrigerate 15 to 20 minutes or until firm enough to handle. Shape dough into two 6-inch rolls. Wrap rolls in wax paper or plastic wrap; freeze 1 to 2 hours or until firm enough to cut. Cut dough into ¼-inch thick slices. Proceed as directed.

Peanut Butter Cut-Out Cookies

CHOCOLATE CHUNK RASPBERRY BARS

⅓ cup sugar
2 tablespoons butter or
   margarine
2 tablespoons water
1¾ cups (10-oz. pkg.)
   HERSHEY'S Semi-Sweet
   Chocolate Chunks, divided
1 egg
1 teaspoon vanilla extract
⅔ cup all-purpose flour
¼ teaspoon baking powder
¼ teaspoon salt
⅓ cup seedless red raspberry
   preserves
½ cup finely chopped nuts
Pecan halves (optional)

▼ Heat oven to 350°F. Grease 8-inch square baking pan. In medium saucepan, combine sugar, butter and water. Cook over medium heat, stirring constantly, until mixture boils.

▼ Remove from heat; immediately add 1 cup chocolate chunks, stirring until melted. Stir in egg and vanilla. Stir together flour, baking powder and salt; add to chocolate mixture, beating until blended. Stir in remaining ¾ cup chocolate chunks; spread batter into prepared pan.

▼ Place pan in freezer 10 minutes. Stir preserves to soften; spread over chilled batter. Sprinkle chopped nuts over top.

▼ Bake 35 to 40 minutes or until bars begin to pull away from sides of pan. Cool completely in pan on wire rack. Cut into bars. Garnish with pecan halves, if desired.
About 16 bars.

CHUNKY MACADAMIA BARS

¾ cup (1½ sticks) butter or
   margarine, softened
1 cup packed light brown sugar
½ cup granulated sugar
1 egg
1 teaspoon vanilla extract
2¼ cups all-purpose flour
1 teaspoon baking soda
¾ cup coarsley chopped
   macadamia nuts
1¾ cups (10-oz. pkg.)
   HERSHEY'S Semi-Sweet
   Chocolate Chunks, divided
Vanilla Glaze

Vanilla Glaze
1 cup powdered sugar
2 tablespoons milk
½ teaspoon vanilla extract

▼ Heat oven to 375°F. In large mixer bowl, beat butter, brown sugar and granulated sugar until light and fluffy. Add egg and vanilla; beat well. Add flour and baking soda; blend well.

▼ Stir in nuts and 1 cup chocolate chunks; spread into ungreased 13 x 9 x 2-inch baking pan. Sprinkle with remaining ¾ cup chocolate chunks.

▼ Bake 25 to 30 minutes or until golden brown. Cool completely in pan on wire rack. Prepare Vanilla Glaze; drizzle over top. Allow to set. Cut into bars.
About 24 bars.

▼ VANILLA GLAZE: In small bowl, combine powdered sugar, milk and vanilla; stir until smooth.

CALIFORNIA CHOCOLATE BARS

6 tablespoons butter or margarine, softened
½ cup granulated sugar
¼ cup packed light brown sugar
1 egg
1 teaspoon freshly grated orange peel
1 teaspoon vanilla extract
1 cup all-purpose flour
½ teaspoon baking soda
¼ teaspoon salt
½ cup chopped dried apricots
½ cup coarsely chopped walnuts
1 cup HERSHEY'S Semi-Sweet Chocolate Chunks
Semi-Sweet Chocolate Glaze

Semi-Sweet Chocolate Glaze
¼ cup HERSHEY'S Semi-Sweet Chocolate Chunks
¾ teaspoon shortening (do not use butter, margarine or oil)

▼ Heat oven to 350°F. Grease 9-inch square baking pan. In large mixer bowl, beat butter, granulated sugar, brown sugar and egg until light and fluffy. Add orange peel and vanilla; blend well.

▼ Stir together flour, baking soda and salt; add to butter mixture. Stir in apricots, walnuts and chocolate chunks; spread into prepared pan.

▼ Bake 25 to 30 minutes or until lightly browned and bars begin to pull away from sides of pan. Cool completely in pan on wire rack. Prepare Semi-Sweet Chocolate Glaze; drizzle over top. Allow to set; cut into bars.
About 16 bars.

▼ SEMI-SWEET CHOCOLATE GLAZE: In small microwave-safe bowl, place chocolate chunks and shortening. Microwave at HIGH (100%) 45 seconds or until chunks are melted and mixture is smooth when stirred.

Chocolate Chunk Raspberry Bars, Chunky Macadamia Bars, California Chocolate Bars

HERSHEY'S GREAT AMERICAN CHOCOLATE CHIP COOKIES

2¼ cups all-purpose flour
1 teaspoon baking soda
½ teaspoon salt
1 cup (2 sticks) butter, softened
¾ cup granulated sugar
¾ cup packed light brown sugar
1 teaspoon vanilla extract
2 eggs
2 cups (12-oz. pkg.)
   HERSHEY'S Semi-Sweet
   Chocolate Chips
1 cup chopped nuts (optional)

▼ Heat oven to 375°F. In bowl, stir together flour, baking soda and salt. In large mixer bowl, beat butter, granulated sugar, brown sugar and vanilla until creamy. Add eggs; beat well. Gradually add flour mixture, beating well.

▼ Stir in chocolate chips and nuts, if desired. Drop by rounded teaspoonfuls onto ungreased cookie sheet.

▼ Bake 9 to 11 minutes or until lightly browned. Cool slightly; remove from cookie sheet to wire rack. Cool completely.
About 6 dozen cookies.

▼ **Variations**
PAN RECIPE
Spread batter in greased 15½ x 10½ x 1-inch jelly roll pan. Bake at 375°F 20 minutes or until lightly browned. Cool completely; cut into bars.
About 4 dozen bars.

SKOR & CHOCOLATE CHIP COOKIES
Use 1 cup finely chopped SKOR Toffee Bars and 1 cup HERSHEY'S Semi-Sweet Chocolate Chips in place of 2 cups chocolate chips; omit nuts. Drop and bake as directed.

ICE CREAM SANDWICH
Press one small scoop vanilla ice cream between two cookies.

Hershey's Great American Chocolate Chip Cookies

JAM-FILLED COCOA COOKIES

¾ cup (1½ sticks) butter or
  margarine, softened
1 can (14 oz.) sweetened
  condensed milk
2 eggs
2 teaspoons vanilla extract
2¾ cups all-purpose flour
⅔ cup HERSHEY'S Cocoa
2 teaspoons baking powder
½ teaspoon baking soda
½ cup ground almonds
Apricot or raspberry preserves
  or jam
Powdered sugar (optional)

▼ In large mixer bowl, beat butter, sweetened condensed milk, eggs and vanilla until well blended. Stir together flour, cocoa, baking powder and baking soda; gradually add to butter mixture, beating until well blended. Stir in almonds.

▼ Divide dough into fourths; wrap each in plastic wrap. Refrigerate about 3 hours. Heat oven to 350°F. Grease cookie sheet.

▼ Working with one portion of dough at a time, (keep remaining portions in refrigerator), on floured surface roll dough ⅛ inch thick.

▼ Cut into an equal number of 2-inch rounds. Place half the rounds onto prepared cookie sheet. Spread about ¼ teaspoon preserves in center of each round.

▼ Using 1-inch round or star-shaped cookie cutter, cut out center portion of remaining half of rounds. Place cut-out rounds on filled rounds; press edges together lightly.

▼ Bake 6 minutes or until set. Remove from cookie sheet to wire rack. Cool completely. Sprinkle powdered sugar over top, if desired.
About 5½ dozen cookies.

1 Cut rolled cookie dough with cookie cutters to make bottom and top layers of cookies.

2 Place solid rounds of cookie dough on cookie sheet and top with preserves.

3 Place the remaining rounds on top of preserves and press edges to seal cookies.

Cocoa Pecan Crescents

**1 cup (2 sticks) butter or
 margarine, softened**
⅔ cup granulated sugar
1½ teaspoons vanilla extract
1¾ cups all-purpose flour
⅓ cup HERSHEY'S Cocoa
⅛ teaspoon salt
1½ cups ground pecans
Powdered sugar

▼ In large mixer bowl, beat butter, granulated sugar and vanilla until light and fluffy. Stir together flour, cocoa and salt; gradually add to butter mixture, blending well. Stir in pecans.

▼ Cover; refrigerate at least 1 hour. Heat oven to 375°F. For each cookie, shape scant 1 tablespoon dough into log, about 2½ inches long; place on ungreased cookie sheet. Shape each log into crescent shape, tapering ends.

▼ Bake 13 to 15 minutes or until set. Cool slightly; remove from cookie sheet to wire rack. Cool completely. Roll in powdered sugar.
About 3½ dozen cookies.

Jam-Filled Cocoa Cookies, Cocoa Pecan Crescents

Double Decker Black & White Brownies

2 cups all-purpose flour
1 teaspoon baking powder
¼ teaspoon salt
1 cup (2 sticks) butter or
  margarine, softened
2 cups packed light brown sugar
2 teaspoons vanilla extract
3 eggs
⅔ HERSHEY'S Semi-Sweet
  Chocolate Chips
⅓ cup HERSHEY'S Cocoa or
  HERSHEY'S European
  Style Cocoa
2 tablespoons vegetable oil
⅔ cup HERSHEY'S Vanilla
  Milk Chips
Vanilla Chip Drizzle

Vanilla Chip Drizzle
⅓ cup HERSHEY'S Vanilla
  Milk Chips
½ teaspoon shortening

▼ Heat oven to 350°F. Grease and flour 13 x 9 x 2-inch baking pan. Stir together flour, baking powder and salt; set aside.

▼ In large mixer bowl, beat butter, brown sugar and vanilla until creamy; add eggs, beating well. Stir in flour mixture until well blended; divide batter in half.

▼ Stir chocolate chips into one part; spread into prepared pan. Into remaining batter, stir cocoa, oil and vanilla milk chips; spread gently and evenly over vanilla layer.

▼ Bake 35 to 40 minutes or until brownies begin to pull away from side of pan. Cool completely in pan on wire rack; cut into bars. Using tines of fork, drizzle Vanilla Chip Drizzle over top of bars; let stand until firm.
About 36 brownies.

▼ VANILLA CHIP DRIZZLE: In small microwave-safe bowl, place vanilla milk chips and shortening. Microwave at HIGH (100%) 30 seconds; stir vigorously. If necessary, microwave at HIGH additional 15 seconds until chips are melted when stirred. Use immediately.

Chocolate Oatmeal Marble Squares

½ cup (1 stick) butter or
  margarine, softened
⅓ cup granulated sugar
⅓ cup packed light brown sugar
1 teaspoon vanilla extract
1 egg
¾ cup all-purpose flour
½ teaspoon baking soda
½ teaspoon salt
1½ cups quick-cooking oats
½ cup HERSHEY'S Butterscotch
  Chips or REESE'S Peanut
  Butter Chips
¾ cup HERSHEY'S Semi-Sweet
  Chocolate Chips

▼ Heat oven to 375°F. Grease 9-inch square baking pan. In large mixer bowl, beat butter, granulated sugar, brown sugar and vanilla until creamy; beat in egg until well blended.

▼ Stir together flour, baking soda and salt; blend into butter mixture. Stir in oats and butterscotch chips. Spread into prepared pan; sprinkle chocolate chips on top.

▼ Bake 3 minutes; leave oven on. With spatula, swirl softened chips in marbled pattern; return to oven.

▼ Bake an additional 15 to 20 minutes or until set. Cool completely in pan on wire rack. Cut into bars.
About 16 bars.

ℬROWNIE CARAMEL PECAN BARS

½ cup sugar
2 tablespoons butter or margarine
2 tablespoons water
2 cups (12-oz. pkg.) HERSHEY'S Semi-Sweet Chocolate Chips, divided
2 eggs, slightly beaten
1 teaspoon vanilla extract
⅔ cup all-purpose flour
¼ teaspoon baking soda
¼ teaspoon salt
Caramel Topping
1 cup pecan pieces

Caramel Topping
25 caramels
¼ cup (½ stick) butter or margarine
2 tablespoons milk

▼ Heat oven to 350°F. Line 9-inch square baking pan with foil; grease and flour foil. In medium saucepan, place sugar, butter and water; cook over low heat, stirring constantly, until mixture boils. Remove from heat; immediately add 1 cup chocolate chips, stirring until melted. Beat in eggs and vanilla until well blended. Stir together flour, baking soda and salt; stir into chocolate mixture. Spread into prepared pan.

▼ Bake 15 to 20 minutes or until brownies begin to pull away from sides of pan. Remove from oven; immediately and carefully spread Caramel Topping over top of brownie. Sprinkle remaining 1 cup chips and pecans over topping. Cool completely in pan on wire rack, being careful not to disturb chips while soft. Cut into bars.
About 16 bars.

▼ CARAMEL TOPPING: Remove wrappers from caramels. In medium microwave-safe bowl, place butter, caramels and milk. Microwave at HIGH (100%) 1 minute; stir. Microwave additional 1 to 2 minutes, stirring every 30 seconds, or until caramels are melted and mixture is smooth when stirred. Use immediately.

Chocolate Oatmeal Marble Squares, Double Decker Black & White Brownies, Brownie Caramel Pecan Bars

HERSHEY'S PREMIUM DOUBLY CHOCOLATE COOKIES

1 cup (2 sticks) butter or margarine, softened
1½ cups sugar
2 eggs
2 teaspoons vanilla extract
2 cups all-purpose flour
⅔ cup HERSHEY'S Cocoa
¾ teaspoon baking soda
¼ teaspoon salt
1¾ cups (10-oz. pkg.) HERSHEY'S Semi-Sweet Chocolate Chunks
½ cup coarsely chopped nuts (optional)

▼ Heat oven to 350°F. In large mixer bowl, beat butter, sugar, eggs and vanilla until light and fluffy. Stir together flour, cocoa, baking soda and salt; add to butter mixture.

▼ Stir in chocolate chunks and nuts, if desired. Drop by tablespoonfuls onto ungreased cookie sheet.

▼ Bake 8 to 10 minutes or just until set. Cool slightly; remove from cookie sheet to wire rack. Cool completely. *About 3 ½ dozen cookies.*

PEANUT BUTTER CHIP COOKIES

1 cup shortening or ¾ cup (1½ sticks) butter or margarine, softened
1 cup granulated sugar
½ cup packed light brown sugar
1 teaspoon vanilla extract
2 eggs
2 cups all-purpose flour
1 teaspoon baking soda
1⅔ cups (10-oz. pkg.) REESE'S Peanut Butter Chips

▼ Heat oven to 350°F. In large mixer bowl, beat shortening, granulated sugar, brown sugar and vanilla until light and fluffy. Add eggs; beat well.

▼ Stir together flour and baking soda. Gradually add flour mixture to sugar mixture, beating well. Stir in peanut butter chips. Drop by rounded teaspoonfuls onto ungreased cookie sheet.

▼ Bake 10 to 12 minutes or until lightly browned. Cool slightly; remove from cookie sheet to wire rack. Cool completely. *About 5 dozen cookies.*

CHEWY CHOCOLATE MACAROONS

5⅓ cups flaked coconut
½ cup HERSHEY'S Cocoa
1 can (14 oz.) sweetened
  condensed milk
2 teaspoons vanilla extract
About 24 red candied cherries,
  halved

▼ Heat oven to 350°F. Generously grease cookie sheet. In large bowl, stir together coconut and cocoa; stir in sweetened condensed milk and vanilla until well blended.

▼ Drop by rounded teaspoonfuls onto prepared cookie sheet. Press cherry half into center of each cookie.

▼ Bake 8 to 10 minutes or until almost set. Immediately remove from cookie sheet to wire rack. Cool completely. Store loosely covered at room temperature.
About 4 dozen cookies.

Chewy Chocolate Macaroons, Hershey's Premium Doubly Chocolate Cookies, Peanut Butter Chip Cookies

Neapolitan Ice Cream Sandwich Cake

1 frozen pound cake loaf
  (10¾ oz.), partially thawed
2 cups (1 pt.) vanilla ice cream,
  slightly softened and divided
2 tablespoons HERSHEY'S
  Strawberry Syrup
2 tablespoons HERSHEY'S
  Syrup

▼ Remove cake from foil pan; line pan with plastic wrap. With serrated knife, slice cake horizontally into 3 layers; place bottom cake layer back into prepared pan and place in freezer.

▼ In small bowl, stir together 1 cup ice cream and strawberry syrup; spread over cake layer in pan. Gently place second cake layer on top of strawberry mixture; immediately return to freezer.

▼ In small bowl, stir together remaining 1 cup ice cream and chocolate syrup; spread over cake layer in pan. Top with third cake layer.

▼ Cover; freeze until firm. Serve frozen, cut into slices. Cover; freeze leftover cake.
About 8 servings.

Frozen Fudge Sundae Dessert

2¼ cups (about 60 crackers)
  finely crushed round
  buttery crackers
½ cup (1 stick) butter or
  margarine, melted
1 jar (about 18 oz.) HERSHEY'S
  Chocolate Shoppe Topping
  (Banana Split Fudge,
  Butterscotch Caramel Fudge,
  Chocolate Caramel Fudge,
  Chocolate Almond Fudge, or
  Double Chocolate Fudge)
2 packages (4-serving size)
  instant vanilla pudding and pie
  filling mix
1½ cups cold milk
4 cups (1 qt.) vanilla ice cream,
  slightly softened
3½ cups (8 oz.) frozen non-dairy
  whipped topping, thawed
12 to 15 maraschino cherries,
  drained (optional)

▼ In 13 x 9 x 2-inch pan, stir together crushed crackers and butter; press onto bottom of pan. Carefully spread fudge topping over crust.

▼ In large bowl, stir together instant pudding mix, milk and ice cream until well blended; spread over mixture in pan. Top with whipped topping.

▼ Cover; freeze until firm, several hours or overnight. Serve frozen; garnish each piece with cherry, if desired. Cover, freeze leftover dessert.
12 to 15 servings.

▼ Variation
FROZEN HOT FUDGE SUNDAE DESSERT
(Since the Hot Fudge flavor of Chocolate Shoppe Topping is thicker than the other varieties, follow these directions.) Prepare crust as directed above. Place open jar HERSHEY'S Hot Fudge Chocolate Shoppe Topping in microwave oven; heat as directed on label. Carefully spread warm fudge topping on top of crust. Prepare, freeze, serve and store dessert as directed above.

Neapolitan Ice Cream Cake, Frozen Fudge Sundae Dessert

PEANUT BUTTER SHELLS WITH CHOCOLATE-ALMOND CREAM

1²⁄₃ **cups (10-oz. pkg.) REESE'S Peanut Butter Chips**
1 tablespoon plus 2 teaspoons shortening (do not use butter, margarine or oil)
Chocolate-Almond Cream Filling

Chocolate-Almond Cream Filling
1 HERSHEY'S Milk Chocolate Bar With Almonds (7 oz.)
1½ cups miniature marshmallows or 15 large marshmallows
⅓ cup milk
1 cup (½ pt.) cold whipping cream

▼ Paper-line 12 muffin cups (2½ inches in diameter). In microwave-safe bowl, place peanut butter chips and shortening. Microwave at HIGH (100%) 1½ minutes or until smooth when stirred.

▼ With narrow pastry brush, thickly and evenly coat inside pleated surface and bottom of each paper cup with peanut butter mixture.

▼ Refrigerate coated cups 10 minutes; recoat any thin spots. (If necessary, microwave peanut butter mixture 30 seconds to thin.) Tightly cover cups; refrigerate until firm.

▼ Remove only a few peanut butter shells from refrigerator at a time; carefully peel paper from each cup. (Will keep weeks in an airtight container in refrigerator.) Fill each cup with Chocolate-Almond Cream Filling; refrigerate several hours or overnight. *12 cups.*

▼ CHOCOLATE-ALMOND CREAM FILLING: With knife, chop chocolate bar into small pieces. In microwave-safe bowl, place marshmallows and milk. Microwave at HIGH 1 minute; stir until marshmallows are melted. Add chocolate; stir until melted. Cool slightly, about 5 minutes. In small mixer bowl, beat whipping cream until stiff. Fold whipped cream into melted chocolate mixture.

Marbled Mocha Squares

1 cup graham cracker crumbs

¼ cup HERSHEY'S Cocoa

¼ cup sugar

¼ cup (½ stick) butter or margarine, melted

4 teaspoons powdered instant coffee

1 tablespoon hot water

1 can (14 oz.) sweetened condensed milk

⅔ cup plus ¼ cup HERSHEY'S Syrup, divided

1 cup chopped walnuts

2 cups (1 pt.) cold whipping cream, whipped

▼ In 9-inch square pan, stir together graham cracker crumbs, cocoa and sugar. Add butter; blend well. Press crumbs firmly onto bottom of pan; set aside.

▼ In large bowl, dissolve coffee in hot water. Add sweetened condensed milk and ⅔ cup syrup; blend well.

▼ Fold in nuts and whipped cream; pour into prepared pan. Drizzle ¼ cup syrup over mixture; with knife or spatula, gently swirl for marbled effect.

▼ Cover; freeze 6 hours or until firm. Cut into squares; garnish as desired. Serve immediately.
9 to 12 servings.

Marbled Mocha Squares, Peanut Butter Shells with Chocolate-Almond Cream

STRAWBERRY-CHOCOLATE BAVARIAN CREAM

1 package (10 oz.) frozen sliced
  strawberries, thawed, or 1 cup
  sweetened, sliced fresh
  strawberries
2 envelopes unflavored gelatin
½ cup sugar
1 cup HERSHEY'S Semi-Sweet
  Chocolate Chips
2¼ cups milk, divided
1 teaspoon vanilla extract
1 cup (½ pt.) cold whipping
  cream
Strawberry Cream

Strawberry Cream
1 cup (½ pt.) cold whipping
  cream
1 teaspoon vanilla extract
2 to 3 drops red food color

▼ Lightly oil 6-cup ring mold. Drain strawberries; reserve syrup. Add water to syrup to equal ¾ cup. Sprinkle gelatin over liquid; let stand 3 minutes. Refrigerate drained berries for use in Strawberry Cream.

▼ In medium saucepan, combine sugar, chocolate chips and ½ cup milk; cook over low heat, stirring constantly, until mixture is smooth and very hot. Add gelatin mixture, stirring until gelatin is completely dissolved.

▼ Remove from heat; add remaining 1¾ cups milk and vanilla. Pour into bowl; refrigerate, stirring occasionally, until mixture mounds when dropped from spoon.

▼ In small mixer bowl, beat whipping cream until stiff; fold into chocolate mixture. Pour into prepared mold; refrigerate until firm, about 2 hours. Unmold; garnish with Strawberry Cream.
8 to 10 servings.

▼ STRAWBERRY CREAM: Mash or puree reserved strawberries to equal ½ cup. In small mixer bowl, beat whipping cream and vanilla until stiff. Fold in strawberry puree and red food color.

CREAMY CHOCOLATE DIPPED STRAWBERRIES

1 cup HERSHEY'S Semi-Sweet
  Chocolate Chips
½ cup HERSHEY'S Vanilla
  Milk Chips
1 tablespoon shortening (do not
  use butter, margarine or oil)
Fresh strawberries, rinsed and
  patted dry (about 2 pts.)

▼ Cover tray with wax paper. In medium microwave-safe bowl, place chocolate chips, vanilla milk chips and shortening. Microwave at HIGH (100%) 1 minute; stir. If necessary, microwave at HIGH additional 30 seconds or until chips are melted and mixture is smooth when stirred vigorusly.

▼ Holding by top, dip bottom two-thirds of each strawberry into melted mixture; shake gently to remove excess. Place on prepared tray.

▼ Cover; refrigerate until coating is firm, about 1 hour. Cover; refrigerate leftover dipped berries. For best results, use within 24 hours.
About 3 dozen coated berries.

Strawberry-Chocolate Bavarian Cream, Creamy Chocolate Dipped Strawberries

CHOCOLATE-FILLED CREAM PUFFS

Chocoalte-Filled Cream Puffs

1 cup water
½ cup (1 stick) butter or margarine
¼ teaspoon salt
1 cup all-purpose flour
4 eggs
Chocolate Cream Filling
Chocolate Glaze

▼ Heat oven to 400°F. In medium saucepan, heat water, butter and salt to rolling boil. Add flour all at once; stir vigorously over low heat about 1 minute or until mixture leaves side of pan and forms a ball.

▼ Remove from heat; add eggs, one at a time, beating well after each addition until smooth and velvety. Drop batter by spoonfuls into 12 balls onto ungreased cookie sheet.

▼ Bake 35 to 40 minutes or until puffed and golden brown. While puff is warm, horizontally slice off small portion of top; reserve tops. Remove any soft piece of dough from inside of puff; cool completely on wire rack.
(continued)

Chocolate Cream Filling
1¼ cups sugar
⅓ cup HERSHEY'S Cocoa
⅓ cup cornstarch
¼ teaspoon salt
3 cups milk
3 egg yolks, slightly beaten
2 tablespoons butter or
margarine
1½ teaspoons vanilla extract

Chocolate Glaze
½ cup HERSHEY'S Semi-Sweet
Chocolate Chips
1 tablespoon shortening (do not
use butter, margarine or oil)

▼ Fill puffs with Chocolate Cream Filling. Replace tops; drizzle with Chocolate Glaze. Refrigerate until serving time. Cover; refrigerate leftover puffs. *About 12 servings.*

▼ CHOCOLATE CREAM FILLING: In medium saucepan, stir together sugar, cocoa, cornstarch and salt; stir in milk. Cook over medium heat, stirring constantly, until mixture boils; boil and stir 1 minute. Remove from heat; gradually stir about 1 cup hot mixture into beaten egg yolks. Return all egg mixture to saucepan. Cook over low heat, stirring constantly, just until mixture comes to a boil. Remove from heat; stir in butter and vanilla;. Pour into bowl; press plastic wrap directly onto surface. Refrigerate 1 to 2 hours or until cold. Do *not* stir. *About 3 cups filling.*

▼ CHOCOLATE GLAZE: In small bowl, place chocolate chips and shortening. Microwave at HIGH (100%) 30 seconds; stir. If necessary, microwave at HIGH additional 15 seconds at a time, stirring after each heating, just until chips are melted when stirred.

1 Cream puff batter is ready when the eggs are thoroughly mixed and mixture is smooth.

2 Drop dough by spoonfuls onto cookie sheet.

3 After baking, cool puffs. Cut open and fill with prepared filling. Puffs may be garnished, if desired.

CHOCOLATE ALMOND CARAMEL TART

½ cup (1 stick) butter or
  margarine, softened
¾ cup sugar, divided
4 eggs
1¼ cups all-purpose flour
½ cup ground toasted almonds*
28 caramels
2 tablespoons water
½ cup (1 stick) butter or
  margarine, melted
¼ cup HERSHEY'S European
  Style Cocoa or HERSHEY'S
  Cocoa
¾ cup light corn syrup
½ teaspoon vanilla extract
½ teaspoon salt
1 cup sliced almonds
Sweetened whipped cream
  (optional)

▼ Heat oven to 350°F. In small mixer bowl, beat ½ cup softened butter and ¼ cup sugar until light and fluffy; blend in 1 egg. Gradually beat in flour until smooth; stir in ground almonds. Press mixture onto bottom and up sides of 11-inch round tart pan with removable bottom.

▼ Remove wrappers from caramels. In small saucepan over low heat, melt caramels with water until melted and smooth; immediately spread on bottom of crust.

▼ In small mixer bowl, beat ½ cup melted butter, remaining ½ cup sugar and cocoa. Add corn syrup, remaining 3 eggs, vanilla and salt; beat until smooth. Pour into crust. Sprinkle sliced almonds over top, leaving 1 inch from outer edge uncovered.

▼ Bake 55 to 60 minutes or until center has started to firm and cracks begin to form along outer edges. (Tart will puff and then fall as it cools.) Cool completely. Cover; refrigerate. Serve with sweetened whipped cream, if desired.
12 to 16 servings.

* To toast almonds: Spread ½ cup almonds on cookie sheet. Bake at 350°F, stirring occasionally, until lightly browned, 8 to 10 minutes; cool.

CHOCOLATE SQUARES WITH NUTTY CARAMEL SAUCE

1 cup sugar
¾ cup all-purpose flour
½ cup HERSHEY'S European
  Style Cocoa or HERSHEY'S
  Cocoa
½ teaspoon baking powder
½ teaspoon salt
¾ cup vegetable oil

▼ Heat oven to 350°F. Grease bottom only of 8-inch square baking pan. In small mixer bowl, stir together sugar, flour, cocoa, baking powder and salt. Add oil, milk, eggs and vanilla; beat until smooth.

▼ Pour batter into prepared pan. Bake 35 to 40 minutes or until wooden pick inserted in center comes out clean. Cool.
(continued)

¼ cup milk
3 eggs
½ teaspoon vanilla extract
1 bag (14 oz.) caramels
½ cup water
1 cup pecan pieces
Sweetened whipped cream
  (optional)

▼ Remove wrappers from caramels. In small saucepan, place caramels and water. Cook over low heat, stirring occasionally, until smooth and well blended. Stir in pecans; cool until thickened slightly.

▼ Cut cake into squares; serve with warm caramel nut sauce and sweetened whipped cream, if desired. *9 servings.*

Chocolate Almond Caramel Tart, Chocolate Squares with Nutty Caramel Sauce

CHOCOLATE SUNDAE PIZZA

⅔ cup shortening
1 cup packed light brown sugar
1 egg
1¾ cups all-purpose flour
¼ teaspoon ground cinnamon
¼ teaspoon salt
½ cup HERSHEY'S Syrup
1 quart ice cream (any flavor)
Sliced fresh fruit
Chocolate Caramel Sauce

Chocolate Caramel Sauce
20 caramels
½ cup HERSHEY'S Syrup
3 tablespoons milk
2 tablespoons butter

▼ Heat oven to 375°F. Grease 12-inch pizza pan. In large mixer bowl, beat shortening and brown sugar until light and fluffy. Add egg; blend well.

▼ Stir together flour, cinnamon and salt; add to shortening mixture alternately with syrup, blending well. Pat dough evenly into prepared pan, forming a slightly thicker edge toward outside of pan. Bake 15 to 17 minutes or until top springs back when touched lightly. Cool completely.

▼ Cut into wedges; do not remove from pan. Place scoop ice cream on each wedge. Arrange fruit around ice cream. Top with Chocolate Caramel Sauce. Serve immediately.
12 servings

▼ CHOCOLATE CARAMEL SAUCE: Remove wrappers from caramels. In small microwave-safe bowl, place caramels, chocolate syrup, milk and butter. Microwave at HIGH (100%) 2 to 2½ minutes or until caramels are softened. Stir until caramels are melted and mixture is blended. If necessary, microwave at HIGH additional 10 seconds; stir until caramels are melted.

CHOCOLATE CINNAMON DESSERT

1⅓ cups all-purpose biscuit baking mix
¾ cup sugar
⅓ cup HERSHEY'S Cocoa
½ teaspoon ground cinnamon
3 tablespoons butter or margarine, softened
¾ cup milk, divided
1 egg
Vanilla ice cream
Chocolate Cinnamon Sauce

Chocolate Cinnamon Sauce
1 cup HERSHEY'S Syrup
¼ teaspoon ground cinnamon

▼ Heat oven to 350°F. Grease and flour 8-inch square baking pan. In large mixer bowl, combine baking mix, sugar, cocoa, cinnamon, butter, ¼ cup milk and egg; beat on medium speed of electric mixer 1 minute. Add remaining ½ cup milk; blend well. Pour batter into prepared pan.

▼ Bake 30 to 35 minutes or until wooden pick inserted in center come out clean. Serve warm or cool topped with ice cream and Chocolate Cinnamon Sauce.
6 to 8 servings.

▼ CHOCOLATE CINNAMON SAUCE: In small bowl, stir together syrup and cinnamon.

Chocolate Sundae Pizza

CHOCOLATE NUT APPLE STRUDEL

1 sheet (½ of 17½ oz. pkg.) frozen puff pastry
1 cup finely shredded peeled apple
¾ cup ground pecans
½ cup (about 15 wafers) vanilla wafer crumbs
¼ cup HERSHEY'S European Style Cocoa or HERSHEY'S Cocoa
¼ cup (½ stick) butter or margarine, melted
⅓ cup sugar
2 eggs
½ teaspoon vanilla extract
2 teaspoons water
Powdered Sugar Glaze
Chocolate Chip Drizzle

Powdered Sugar Glaze
¾ cup powdered sugar
½ to 1 tablespoon milk

Chocolate Chip Drizzle
¼ cup HERSHEY'S Semi-Sweet Chocolate Chips
1½ teaspoons shortening (do not use butter, margarine or oil)

▼ Thaw puff pastry according to package directions. Heat oven to 425°F. Sprinkle cookie sheet with cold water; set aside.

▼ In medium bowl, stir together apple, pecans, crumbs and cocoa. In small bowl, combine butter, sugar, 1 egg and vanilla; add to cocoa mixture. Blend well.

▼ With floured rolling pin, roll pastry on lightly floured surface to 12 x 10-inch rectangle. Place filling down center of pastry. Combine remaining 1 egg and water.

▼ Fold left side of pastry over filling; brush long edge with egg mixture. Brush long edge of remaining pastry with egg mixture. Fold over filling; press edges together to seal. Place seam-side down on prepared cookie sheet. Brush with remaining egg mixture.

▼ Bake 20 to 25 minutes or until golden brown. Cool. Prepare Powdered Sugar Glaze; drizzle over strudel. Prepare Chocolate Chip Drizzle; drizzle over strudel. Cut into slices.
10 to 12 servings.

▼ POWDERED SUGAR GLAZE: In small bowl, stir together powdered sugar and milk until smooth.

▼ CHOCOLATE CHIP DRIZZLE: In small microwave-safe bowl, place chocolate chips and shortening. Microwave at HIGH (100%) 30 seconds; stir. If necessary, microwave at HIGH an additional 30 seconds or until chocolate is melted and mixture is smooth when stirred.

PEANUT BUTTER AND APPLE CRUMBLE

4 cups thinly sliced, peeled apples

1⅔ cups (10-oz. pkg.) REESE'S Peanut Butter Chips

1 cup sugar, divided

2 tablespoons plus ½ cup all-purpose flour, divided

6 tablespoons butter or margarine, divided

1 cup quick-cooking or regular rolled oats

½ teaspoon ground cinnamon

Whipped cream (optional)

▼ Heat oven to 350°F. Grease 9-inch square baking pan. In large bowl, stir together apples, peanut butter chips, ¾ cup sugar and 2 tablespoons flour. Spread into prepared pan; dot with 2 tablespoons butter.

▼ Combine oats, remaining ½ cup flour, remaining ¼ cup sugar, remaining 4 tablespoons butter and cinnamon until crumbs form. Sprinkle crumb mixture over apples.

▼ Bake 40 to 45 minutes or until apples are tender and edges are bubbly. Cool slightly. Serve warm with whipped cream, if desired.
6 to 8 servings.

Chocolate Nut Apple Strudel, Peanut Butter and Apple Crumble

Chocolate Syrup Swirl Dessert, Chocolate Syrup Mint Mousse

Chocolate Syrup Swirl Dessert

1 envelope unflavored gelatin
¼ cup cold water
1 package (8 oz.) cream cheese, softened
¼ cup sugar
1 teaspoon vanilla extract
¾ cup HERSHEY'S Syrup, chilled
¾ cup milk
Vanilla Filling
Crumb Crust

Vanilla Filling
1 teaspoon unflavored gelatin
1 tablespoon cold water
2 tablespoons boiling water
1 cup (½ pt.) cold whipping cream
2 tablespoons sugar
½ teaspoon vanilla extract

Crumb Crust
2 cups (about 60 wafers) vanilla wafer crumbs or graham cracker crumbs
⅓ cup butter or margarine, melted

▼ In small saucepan, sprinkle gelatin over water; let stand 2 minutes. Cook over low heat, stirring constantly, until gelatin is dissolved.

▼ In large mixer bowl, beat cream cheese, sugar and vanilla until creamy. Add syrup, gelatin mixture and milk; blend well. Refrigerate, stirring occasionally, until mixture mounds from spoon, about 20 minutes.

▼ Spoon one-half chocolate mixture into crust; top with one-half Vanilla Filling. Repeat procedure, ending with dollops of Vanilla Filling on top. With knife or metal spatula, gently swirl through dessert.

▼ Cover; refrigerate several hours until set. (Dessert is best served same day as prepared.)
10 to 12 servings.

▼ VANILLA FILLING: In small cup, sprinkle gelatin over cold water; let stand 1 minute. Add boiling water; stir until gelatin is completely dissolved; cool slightly. In small mixer bowl, combine whipping cream, sugar and vanilla; beat until slightly thickened.Gradually add gelatin mixture; beat until stiff.

▼ CRUMB CRUST: In bowl, stir together crumbs and butter. Press mixture onto bottom and 1½ inches up side of 9-inch springform pan or 10-inch pie plate. Refrigerate about 30 minutes or until firm.

Chocolate Syrup Mint Mousse

1 teaspoon unflavored gelatin
1 tablespoon cold water
2 tablespoons boiling water
1 cup (½ pt.) cold whipping cream
½ cup HERSHEY'S Syrup, chilled
2 to 3 drops mint extract
Sweetened whipped cream
Sliced fresh fruit

▼ In small cup, sprinkle gelatin over cold water; let stand 2 minutes. Add boiling water, stirring until gelatin is completely dissolved.

▼ In small mixer bowl, beat whipping cream until slightly thickened; gradually add gelatin mixture, beating until stiff. Fold in syrup and mint extract.

▼ Spoon into individual dessert dishes. Refrigerate 30 minutes or until set. Garnish with sweetened whipped cream and fruit.
About 4 servings.

CHOCOLATE TORTONI

1 cup (½ pt.) cold whipping
  cream
½ cup cold HERSHEY'S Syrup
¼ cup almond macaroon or
  vanilla wafer crumbs
¼ cup chopped, toasted
  almonds*
¼ cup chopped maraschino
  cherries
1 tablespoon plus 1 ½ teaspoons
  rum or ½ teaspoon rum extract
Chocolate-dipped maraschino
  cherries (optional)
Sliced almonds (optional)

▼ In small mixer bowl, beat whipping cream until stiff; gently fold in syrup. Stir in almond macaroon crumbs, ¼ cup chopped almonds, chopped maraschino cherries and rum.

▼ Spoon mixture into 4 dessert dishes; cover and freeze until firm, about 4 hours. Let stand several minutes before serving. Garnish with cherries and almonds; if desired.
4 servings.

* To toast almonds: Spread almonds on cookie sheet. Bake at 350°F, stirring occasionally, until lightly browned, 8 to 10 minutes; cool.

COOKIE ICE CREAM BALLS

10 chocolate sandwich cookies
½ gallon vanilla ice cream
Peanut Butter Sauce

Peanut Butter Sauce
1²⁄₃ cups (10-oz. pkg.) REESE'S
  Peanut Butter Chips
²⁄₃ cup milk
½ cup whipping cream
¼ teaspoon vanilla extract

▼ Line cookie sheet with wax paper; place in freezer. In blender or food processor bowl, crush chocolate sandwich cookies (filling included) to make 1 cup crumbs; pour into shallow dish.

▼ Using large scoop, make eight 2 ½-inch ice cream balls; roll in crumbs. Place on prepared cold cookie sheet. Cover; freeze. Serve ice cream balls with Peanut Butter Sauce.
6 servings.

▼ PEANUT BUTTER SAUCE: In medium saucepan, combine peanut butter chips, milk and whipping cream. Cook over low heat, stirring constantly until chips are melted and mixture is smooth. Remove from heat; stir in vanilla. Serve warm.
About 2 cups sauce.

CHOCOLATE MACADAMIA NUT ICE CREAM

1 can (14 oz.) sweetened condensed milk
½ cup HERSHEY'S European Style Cocoa
2 cups (1 pt.) whipping cream
1 cup (½ pt.) light cream
1 tablespoon vanilla extract
½ cup macadamia nuts, coarsely chopped

▼ In medium saucepan, combine sweetened condensed milk and cocoa. Cook over low heat, stirring constantly, until mixture is smooth and slightly thickened, about 5 minutes.

▼ Remove from heat; cool slightly. Gradually add whipping cream, light cream and vanilla, beating with wire whisk until well blended; refrigerate until mixture is cold.

▼ Pour into 4- or 5-quart ice cream freezer container. Freeze according to manufacturer's directions. Stir in nuts.
About 2 quarts.

Chocolate Macadamia Nut Ice Cream, Cookie Ice Cream Balls, Chocolate Tortoni

SILKEN CHOCOLATE DESSERT WITH CITRUS SAUCE

1 envelope unflavored gelatin
¾ cup sugar
½ cup HERSHEY'S Cocoa
1 cup light cream or
**   half-and-half**
½ cup milk
2 tablespoons butter or
**   margarine, softened**
1 teaspoon vanilla extract
1 cup (½ pt.) cold whipping
**   cream**
Fresh fruit (grapes, nectarines,
**   oranges, raspberries,**
**   strawberries)**
Citrus Sauce

Citrus Sauce
1 cup sugar
2 tablespoons cornstarch
¼ teaspoon salt
1¼ cups orange juice
½ cup water
¼ cup lemon juice
1 tablespoon butter or margarine
½ to 1 teaspoon freshly grated
**   orange peel**
Yellow food color (optional)

▼ In medium saucepan, stir together unflavored gelatin and sugar; add cocoa. Stir in light cream and milk; let stand 1 minute.

▼ Cook over low heat, stirring constantly with whisk, until gelatin is completely dissolved, about 5 minutes.

▼ Remove from heat; stir in butter and vanilla. Pour into large bowl; refrigerate, stirring occasionally, just until mixture begins to thicken, about 1 hour.

▼ In small mixer bowl, beat whipping cream until stiff; fold into gelatin mixture. Pour into 4-cup mold; refrigerate until firm, about 3 hours. To serve, unmold onto serving plate; garnish with fruit. Serve with Citrus Sauce.
8 to 10 servings.

▼ CITRUS SAUCE: In small saucepan, stir together sugar, cornstarch and salt; stir in orange juice, water and lemon juice. Cook over medium heat, stirring constantly, until mixture boils. Boil and stir 3 minutes. Remove from heat; add butter, orange peel and food color, if desired. Cool completely.
About 2 cups sauce.

FAST FUDGE POTS DE CREME

1 package (4-serving size)
**   chocolate cook & serve**
**   pudding and pie filling mix***
2 cups milk
1 cup HERSHEY'S Semi-Sweet
Chocolate Chips or
HERSHEY'S MINI CHIPS
Semi-Sweet Chocolate

▼ In medium saucepan, stir together pudding mix and milk. Cook over medium heat, stirring constantly, until mixture comes to full boil; remove from heat.

▼ Add chocolate chips; stir until chips are melted and mixture is smooth. Spoon into creme pots or demi-tasse cups.

▼ Press plastic wrap directly onto surface. Serve slightly warm or chilled. Garnish as desired.
8 servings.

* Do not use instant pudding mix.

Silken Chocolate Dessert with Citrus Sauce, Fast Fudge Pots de Creme

DEEP DARK CHOCOLATE SOUFFLE

1 tablespoon sugar
½ cup HERSHEY'S European Style Cocoa
¼ cup all-purpose flour
¼ cup (½ stick) butter or margarine, softened
1 cup milk
½ cup plus 2 tablespoons sugar, divided
1 teaspoon vanilla extract
4 eggs, separated
Vanilla ice cream

▼ Heat oven to 350°F. Butter 6-cup souffle dish; coat with 1 tablespoon sugar. In medium bowl, combine cocoa and flour. Add butter; blend well. Set aside. In medium saucepan, heat milk until very hot. Reduce heat; add cocoa mixture, beating with wire whisk until smooth and thick.

▼ Remove from heat; stir in ½ cup sugar and vanilla. Cool slightly. Add egg yolks, one at a time, beating well after each addition. Cool to room temperature.

▼ In large mixer bowl, beat egg whites until foamy; gradually add remaining 2 tablespoons sugar and continue beating until stiff.

▼ Stir small amount beaten whites into chocolate mixture; fold chocolate mixture into remaining whites. Carefully pour into prepared dish.

▼ Bake 40 to 45 minutes until puffed. Serve immediately with ice cream.
6 servings.

Deep Dark Chocolate Souffle

CHOCOLATE KISS MOUSSE

1 ½ cups miniature or 15 regular
   marshmallows
⅓ cup milk
2 teaspoons kirsch (cherry
   brandy) or ¼ teaspoon
   almond extract
6 to 8 drops red food color
36 HERSHEY'S KISSES Milk
   Chocolates
1 cup (½ pt.) cold whipping
   cream
Additional HERSHEY'S KISSES
   Milk Chocolates, (optional)

▼ In small saucepan, combine marshmallows and milk.
Cook over low heat, stirring constantly, until marshmallows are melted and mixture is smooth. Remove
from heat. Into medium bowl, pour ⅓ cup marshmallow mixture; stir in brandy and food color. Set aside.

▼ Remove wrappers from chocolate pieces. To remaining marshmallow mixture, add 36 chocolate
pieces; return to low heat, stirring constantly until
chocolate is melted. Remove from heat; cool to
room temperature.

▼ In small mixer bowl, beat whipping cream until stiff.
Fold 1 cup whipped cream into chocolate mixture.
Gradually fold remaining whipped cream into
reserved mixture.

▼ Fill 4 parfait glasses about three-fourths full with
chocolate mixture; spoon or pipe remaining mixture
on top. Refrigerate 3 to 4 hours or until set. Garnish
with additional chocolate pieces, if desired.
4 servings.

Chocolate Kiss Mousse

Fudgey Fondue

ℱUDGEY FONDUE

2 cups (12-oz. pkg.)
HERSHEY'S Semi-Sweet
Chocolate Chips
¾ cup milk
1 can (14 oz.) sweetened
condensed milk
Assorted Fondue Dippers:
cake pieces, marshmallows,
cherries, grapes, mandarin
orange segments, pineapple
chunks, strawberries, fresh
fruit slices

▼ In heavy saucepan over low heat, combine chocolate chips, milk and sweetened condensed milk. Stir constantly until chocolate is melted and mixture is hot.

▼ Pour into fondue pot or chafing dish; serve warm with Assorted Fondue Dippers.
About 3 cups fondue.

𝒞HOCOLATE LOVER'S FONDUE

2 cups (12-oz. pkg.) HERSHEY'S
Semi-Sweet Chocolate Chips
¾ cup light cream or half-
and-half
½ cup sugar
Assorted Fondue Dippers:
cake pieces, marshmallows,
cherries, grapes, mandarin
orange segments, pineapple
chunks, strawberries, fresh
fruit slices

▼ In heavy saucepan, combine chocolate chips, light cream and sugar. Cook over low heat, stirring constantly, until chocolate is melted and mixture is hot.

▼ Pour into fondue pot or chafing dish; serve warm with Assorted Fondue Dippers.
About 2 cups fondue.

▼ **Variation**
2 tablespoons kirsch (cherry brandy) may be added before serving.

CALIFORNIA STRAWBERRY LOG

California Strawberry Log

3 eggs, separated
½ cup granulated sugar
½ cup all-purpose flour
⅓ cup HERSHEY'S Cocoa
⅓ cup granulated sugar
½ teaspoon baking soda
¼ teaspoon salt
⅓ cup water
1 teaspoon vanilla extract
1 tablespoon granulated sugar

▼ Heat oven to 375°F. Line 15½ x 10½ x 1-inch jelly-roll pan with foil; generously grease foil. In large mixer bowl, beat egg yolks on high speed of electric mixer 3 minutes. Gradually add ½ cup granulated sugar; continue beating 2 minutes.

▼ Stir together flour, cocoa, ⅓ cup granulated sugar, baking soda and salt; add alternately with water and vanilla to egg yolk mixture, beating on low speed just until smooth.
(continued)

**2 tablespoons plus ¾ cup
powdered sugar, divided**
**2 cups (1 pt.) cold whipping
cream**
1 teaspoon vanilla extract
**3 cups sliced fresh strawberries
or two packages (16 oz. each)
frozen strawberries, thawed**
**Additional strawberries, coarsely
chopped (optional)**

▼ In small mixer bowl, beat egg whites until foamy.
Add 1 tablespoon granulated sugar and beat until
stiff peaks form; carefully fold into chocolate mixture.
Spread batter evenly into prepared pan.

▼ Bake 15 to 18 minutes or until top springs back
when touched lightly. Invert on towel sprinkled with
2 tablespoons powdered sugar; carefully remove foil.
Immediately roll cake and towel together from narrow end; place on wire rack to cool.

▼ In clean large mixer bowl, beat whipping cream,
remaining ¾ cup powdered sugar and vanilla on high
speed until stiff.

▼ Fold sliced strawberries into 2 cups whipped cream;
reserve remaining whipped cream for garnish. Unroll
cake and spread with strawberry-cream mixture.
Reroll.

▼ Garnish with reserved whipped cream and chopped
strawberries, if desired. Refrigerate 1 hour or longer
before serving. Refrigerate leftover dessert.
8 to 10 servings.

1 Place baked cake on towel
sprinkled with powdered sugar.
Roll towel and cake together to
form a log.

2 Spread cake with filling.

3 Carefully re-roll cake and
filling.

CHOCOLATE PLUM PUDDING

3 cups (4 to 5 slices) soft white
   bread crumbs
1 cup all-purpose flour
¾ cup sugar
6 tablespoons HERSHEY'S Cocoa
1½ teaspoons baking soda
½ teaspoon salt
½ cup (1 stick) butter or
   margarine, melted
½ cup orange marmalade
¾ cup milk
1 cup raisins
½ cup chopped walnuts or pecans
Hard Sauce

Hard Sauce
1 cup powdered sugar
½ cup butter, softened
1 to 2 tablespoons brandy,
   (optional)
½ teaspoon lemon juice or
   vanilla extract

▼ Thoroughly grease 8-cup mold. In large bowl combine bread crumbs, flour, sugar, cocoa, baking soda and salt. Add butter, mar-malade and milk; blend well. Stir in raisins and nuts.

▼ Spoon butter into prepared mold; cover tightly with lightly greased foil. Place mold on rack in deep kettle. Pour boiling water into kettle to depth of about 1 inch.

▼ Cover; simmer 3 hours. Add water as needed to keep level of about 1 inch. Remove mold from kettle to cooling rack. Cool 5 minutes; invert onto serving plate. Serve warm with Hard Sauce.
10 servings.

▼ HARD SAUCE: In small bowl, beat powdered sugar and butter until well blended. Add brandy, if desired and lemon juice; beat until light and fluffy. Chill thoroughly. Refrigerate until thoroughly chilled.

CHOCOLATE ENGLISH TRIFLE

½ cup apricot preserves
3 tablespoons light rum
16 to 18 ladyfingers, split
Chocolate Filling
Sweetened whipped cream

Chocolate Filling
⅓ cup sugar
3 tablespoons cornstarch
¼ teaspoon salt
2¼ cups milk
⅔ cup HERSHEY'S Syrup
1 egg, well beaten
1 tablespoon butter or margarine
1 teaspoon vanilla extract

▼ Stir together preserves and rum; spread flat side of each ladyfinger with mixture. Put 6 to 8 ladyfingers together sandwich style; arrange on bottom of 1½-quart glass serving bowl. Arrange single ladyfingers around sides of bowl.

▼ Spoon one-half prepared Chocolate Filling into bowl. Arrange single layer of ladyfingers on filling. Top with remaining filling. Cover; refrigerate several hours. Garnish with sweetened whipped cream. Cover; refrigerate leftover dessert.
10 to 12 servings.

▼ CHOCOLATE FILLING: In medium saucepan, combine sugar, cornstarch and salt; gradually stir in milk, syrup and egg. Cook over medium heat, stirring constantly, until mixture boils; boil and stir 1 minute. Remove from heat; blend in butter and vanilla. Pour into bowl; press plastic wrap directly onto surface. Cool; refrigerate about 1 hour.

Chocolate Plum Pudding

Pears au Chocolat

4 fresh ripe pears with stems
1 cup water
½ cup sugar
1 teaspoon vanilla extract
Nut Filling (optional)
Chocolate Sauce
Sweetened whipped cream
    (optional)

Nut Filling
6 tablespoons finely
    chopped nuts
2 tablespoons powdered sugar
1 teaspoon milk

Chocolate Sauce
6 tablespoons sugar
6 tablespoons water
¼ cup (½ stick) butter
1⅓ cups HERSHEY'S MINI
    CHIPS Semi-Sweet Chocolate

▼ Core pears from bottom, leaving stems intact; peel. Cut slice from bottom to make a flat base. In medium saucepan, stir together water and sugar; add pears.

▼ Cover; cook over low heat 10 to 20 minutes or just until pears are soft. (Cooking time will depend on size, type and ripeness of pears.) Remove from heat; add vanilla. Cool pears in syrup; refrigerate.

▼ To serve, drain pears; spoon Nut Filling into cavities. Place pears on dessert plates. Spoon Chocolate Sauce onto each pear. Garnish with whipped cream; if desired.
4 servings.

▼ NUT FILLING: In small bowl, stir together nuts, powdered sugar and milk.

▼ CHOCOLATE SAUCE: In small saucepan, combine sugar, water and butter. Cook over medium heat, stirring constantly, until mixture boils. Remove from heat; stir in small chocolate chips. Stir until chocolate has completely melted; beat or whisk until smooth. Cool.
About 1⅓ cups sauce.

Peanut Butter Chip Apple Cobbler

5 cups sliced, peeled tart cooking apples
1 cup REESE'S Peanut Butter Chips
²/₃ cup sugar
2 tablespoons all-purpose flour
¹/₂ teaspoon ground cinnamon
¹/₄ teaspoon salt
1 teaspoon lemon juice
1 teaspoon vanilla extract
Cobbler Batter
Sweetened Whipped Cream

Cobbler Batter
²/₃ cup all-purpose flour
²/₃ cup sugar
³/₄ teaspoon baking powder
¹/₄ teaspoon salt
¹/₄ cup (¹/₂ stick) butter or margarine, softened
1 egg, slightly beaten

▼ Heat oven to 375°F (325°F for glass baking dish). In large bowl, stir together all ingredients except Cobbler Batter; spoon into ungreased 8-inch square baking pan.

▼ Spoon tablespoonfuls Cobbler Batter evenly over filling in pan (batter will spread during baking).

▼ Bake 45 minutes or until apples are tender and batter is golden brown. Serve with whipped cream, if desired. *8 servings.*

▼ COBBLER BATTER: In large bowl, combine all ingredients; beat with spoon until smooth and well blended.

Peanut Butter Chip Apple Cobbler, Pears au Chocolat

Frosty Chocolate Chip Pie

1 cup HERSHEY'S Semi-Sweet
  Chocolate Chips
⅓ cup milk
1 pkg. (3 oz.) cream cheese,
  softened
2½ cups frozen non-dairy
  whipped topping, thawed
1 baked 8-inch pie crust, cooled
  or packaged crumb crust (6 oz.)
Additional whipped topping
Fresh fruit slices

▼ In medium microwave-safe bowl, combine chocolate chips and milk. Microwave at HIGH (100%) 1½ minutes or until hot.

▼ With wire whisk or spoon, beat in cream cheese until well blended and smooth. Cool just to room temperature.

▼ Gently fold 2½ cups whipped topping into chocolate mixture; spoon into crust. Cover; freeze until firm. Garnish with whipped topping and fresh fruit.
6 to 8 servings.

Brownie Pie a La Mode

½ cup sugar
2 tablespoons butter or
  margarine
2 tablespoons water
1⅓ cups HERSHEY'S Semi-
  Sweet Chocolate Chips
2 eggs
⅔ cup all-purpose flour
¼ teaspoon baking soda
¼ teaspoon salt
1 teaspoon vanilla extract
¾ cup chopped nuts (optional)
Favorite flavor ice cream
Fudge Sauce (optional)

Fudge Sauce
1 cup HERSHEY'S Semi-Sweet
  Chocolate Chips
½ cup evaporated milk
¼ cup sugar
1 tablespoon butter or margarine

▼ Heat oven to 350°F. Grease 9-inch pie plate. In medium saucepan, combine sugar, butter and water. Cook over medium heat, stirring occasionally, just until mixture boils.

▼ Remove from heat; immediately add chocolate chips, stirring until melted. Add eggs; beat with spoon until well-blended.

▼ Stir together flour, baking soda and salt; stir into chocolate mixture. Stir in vanilla and chopped nuts; pour into prepared pie plate.

▼ Bake 25 to 30 minutes or until almost set. (Pie will not test done in center.) Cool completely.

▼ Cut into wedges. Serve topped with scoops of ice cream. Drizzle with Fudge Sauce, if desired.
8 to 10 servings.

▼ FUDGE SAUCE: In medium microwave-safe bowl, combine all ingredients. Microwave at HIGH (100%) 1 to 1½ minutes or until hot. With wire whisk, beat until chips are melted and mixture is smooth.
About 1½ cups sauce.

Frosty Chocolate Chip Pie, Brownie Pie a La Mode

Quick & Easy Chocolate Cheesecake Pie

2 packages (8 oz. each) cream cheese, softened
¾ cup sugar
2 eggs
¼ cup HERSHEY'S Cocoa or HERSHEY'S European Style Cocoa
1½ teaspoons vanilla extract
1 extra serving-size packaged graham cracker crumb crust (9 oz.)
2 cups frozen non-dairy whipped topping, thawed

▼ Heat oven to 350°F. Beat cream cheese and sugar until blended; beat in eggs until well blended. Add cocoa and vanilla, blending until smooth. Pour into crust.

▼ Bake 30 to 35 minutes or until almost set in center. Cool completely on wire rack. Cover; refrigerate. Spread whipped topping over top; garnish as desired. Refrigerate leftover pie.
8 to 10 servings.

Chocolate Mousse and Praline Pie

⅓ cup butter or margarine
¼ cup packed light brown sugar
2 tablespoons water
1 tablespoon cornstarch
⅔ cup coarsely chopped pecans
1 packaged crumb crust (6 oz.)
Chocolate Mousse Filling
Pecan halves

Chocolate Mousse Filling
1 teaspoon unflavored gelatin
1 tablespoon cold water
2 tablespoons boiling water
½ cup sugar
¼ cup HERSHEY'S Cocoa
1 cup (½ pt.) cold whipping cream
1 teaspoon vanilla extract

▼ In small microwave-safe bowl, place butter. Microwave at HIGH (100%) 1 minute or until melted. Add brown sugar, water and cornstarch; stir with wire whisk until smooth.

▼ Microwave at HIGH 1 minute or until mixture comes to full boil. Stir in chopped pecans; spread mixture on bottom of crust. Place crust in freezer.

▼ Prepare Chocolate Mousse Filling. Carefully spread filling over pecan layer. Cover; refrigerate 3 to 4 hours. Garnish with pecan halves. Refrigerate leftover pie.
6 to 8 servings.

▼ CHOCOLATE MOUSSE FILLING: In small cup, sprinkle gelatin over cold water; let stand 1 minute to soften. Add boiling water; stir until gelatin is completely dissolved and mixture is clear. Cool slightly, about 5 minutes. Meanwhile, in small mixer bowl, stir together sugar and cocoa; add whipping cream and vanilla. Beat on medium speed of electric mixer, scraping bottom of bowl occasionally, until stiff. Add gelatin mixture; beat just until well blended.

CHOCOLATE CHIP WALNUT PIE

¾ **cup packed light brown sugar**
½ **cup all-purpose flour**
½ **teaspoon baking powder**
¼ **teaspoon ground cinnamon**
2 eggs, slightly beaten
1 cup HERSHEY'S Semi-Sweet
Chocolate Chips, MINI CHIPS
or Milk Chocolate Chips
1 cup coarsely chopped walnuts
1 baked 9-inch pie crust, cooled
Spiced Cream

Spiced Cream
½ **cup cold whipping cream**
1 tablespoon powdered sugar
¼ **teaspoon vanilla extract**
¼ **teaspoon ground cinnamon**
Dash ground nutmeg

▼ Heat oven to 350°F. In bowl, stir together brown sugar, flour, baking powder and cinnamon. Add eggs; stir until well blended. Stir in chocolate chips and walnuts. Pour into baked pie crust.

▼ Bake 25 to 30 minutes or until lightly browned and set. Serve slightly warm or at room temperature with Spiced Cream.
8 servings.

▼ SPICED CREAM: In small mixer bowl, combine whipping cream, powdered sugar, vanilla, cinnamon and nutmeg; beat until stiff.
About 1 cup topping.

Chocolate Mousse and Praline Pie, Chocolate Chip Walnut Pie

CHOCOLATE STRAWBERRY FRUIT TART

1⅓ cups all-purpose flour
½ cup powdered sugar
1/4 cup HERSHEY'S Cocoa or
   HERSHEY'S European Style
   Cocoa
¾ cup (1½ sticks) butter or
   margarine, softened
Strawberry Vanilla Filling
½ cup HERSHEY'S Semi-Sweet
   Chocolate Chips
1 tablespoon shortening (do not
   use butter, margarine or oil)
Glazed Fruit Topping

Strawberry Vanilla Filling
1⅔ cups (10-oz. pkg.)
   HERSHEY'S Vanilla Milk
   Chips
¼ cup evaporated milk
1 package (8 oz.) cream cheese,
   softened
1 teaspoon strawberry extract
2 drops red food color

Glazed Fruit Topping
¼ teaspoon unflavored gelatin
1 teaspoon cold water
1½ teaspoons cornstarch
   or arrowroot
¼ cup apricot nectar or orange
   juice
2 tablespoons sugar
½ teaspoon lemon juice
Assorted fresh fruit, sliced

▼ Heat oven to 325°F. Grease and flour 12-inch round pizza pan. In medium bowl, stir together flour, powdered sugar and cocoa. With fork, cut in butter until mixture holds together; press evenly in prepared pan.

▼ Bake 10 to 15 minutes or until crust is set; cool completely. Spread Strawberry Vanilla Filling evenly over crust to within 1 inch of edge; refrigerate until filling is firm.

▼ In small microwave-safe bowl, place chocolate chips and shortening. Microwave at HIGH (100%) 30 seconds to 1 minute or until chocolate is melted when stirred. Spoon chocolate into corner of disposable pastry bag or heavy duty plastic bag; cut off small piece at corner. Squeeze onto outer edge of filling in decorative design; refrigerate until firm.

▼ Prepare Glazed Fruit Topping; place onto top of filling. Refrigerate until ready to serve. Cover; refrigerate leftover tart.
12 servings.

▼ STRAWBERRY VANILLA FILLING: In medium microwave-safe bowl, place vanilla milk chips and evaporated milk. Microwave at HIGH (100%) 1 to 1½ minutes or until chips are melted and mixture is smooth when stirred vigorously. Beat in cream cheese, strawberry extract and food color.

▼ GLAZED FRUIT TOPPING: In small cup, sprinkle gelatin over cold water; let stand several minutes to soften. In small saucepan, stir together cornstarch, apricot nectar, sugar and lemon juice; cook over medium heat, stirring constantly, until mixture is thickened. Remove from heat; immediately stir in gelatin mixture until smooth. Cool slightly. Meanwhile, arrange fruit on top of filling; carefully brush juice mixture over fruit.

Chocolate Strawberry Fruit Tart

Cool 'n Creamy Chocolate Pie

1 package (3 oz.) cream cheese, softened
¼ cup sugar
1 teaspoon vanilla extract
½ cup HERSHEY'S Syrup
1 cup (½ pt.) cold whipping cream
1 packaged crumb crust (6 oz.)
Sliced fresh fruit (optional)
Chocolate curls (optional)

▼ In small mixer bowl, beat cream cheese, sugar and vanilla until well blended. Gradually add syrup, beating until smooth.

▼ In small mixer bowl, beat whipping cream until stiff. Carefully fold into chocolate mixture. Pour into crust. Cover; freeze until firm. Just before serving, garnish with fresh fruit and chocolate curls, if desired. *6 to 8 servings.*

Cool 'n Creamy Chocolate Pie

CHOCOLATE ICE CRISPY PIE

½ cup HERSHEY'S Syrup
⅓ cup HERSHEY'S Semi-Sweet
  Chocolate Chips
2 cups crisp rice cereal
¼ cup dairy sour cream
4 cups (1 qt.) favorite flavor
  ice cream

▼ Butter 8-inch pie plate. In medium microwave-safe bowl, place syrup and chocolate chips. Microwave at HIGH (100%) 45 seconds or until hot; stir until smooth.

▼ Remove ¼ cup chocolate mixture to small bowl. Add cereal to remaining chocolate mixture, stirring until well coated; cool slightly.

▼ Using back of spoon, press mixture evenly on bottom and up sides of prepared pie plate to form crust. Place in freezer 15 to 20 minutes or until crust is firm.

▼ Meanwhile, stir sour cream into reserved chocolate mixture. Spoon half of ice cream into crust; spoon portion of chocolate sauce over layer. Top with scoops of ice cream and remaining sauce. Cover; return to freezer until serving time.
6 servings.

Chocolate Ice Crispy Pie

PEANUT BUTTER CHIP BANANA PIE

⅓ cup sugar
⅓ cup cornstarch
¼ teaspoon salt
2¼ cups milk
2 egg yolks, slightly beaten
1⅔ cups (10-oz. pkg.) REESE'S
  Peanut Butter Chips
1 teaspoon vanilla extract
1 small banana, sliced
1 packaged crumb crust (6 oz.)
Whipped topping (optional)
Banana slices (optional)
Additional REESE'S Peanut
  Butter Chips (optional)

▼ In medium saucepan, stir together sugar, cornstarch and salt; stir in milk. Cook over medium heat, stirring constantly, until mixture boils; boil and stir 1 minute. Remove from heat.

▼ Stir ½ cup cooked mixture into egg yolks. Return mixture to saucepan, stirring until blended.

▼ Cook over low heat, stirring constantly, 2 minutes. Do not boil. Remove from heat. Immediately add peanut butter chips and vanilla; stir until chips are melted and mixture is smooth. Cool 10 minutes.

▼ Meanwhile, arrange banana slices over bottom of crust; pour filling over bananas. Press plastic wrap directly onto surface; refrigerate several hours or overnight. Garnish with whipped topping, banana slices and peanut butter chips, if desired. Cover; refrigerate leftover pie.
6 to 8 servings.

Banana Split Pie, Peanut Butter Chip Banana Pie

ℬANANA SPLIT PIE

1¼ cups sugar
⅓ cup cornstarch
⅓ cup HERSHEY'S Cocoa
¼ teaspoon salt
2½ cups milk
2 egg yolks, slightly beaten
3 tablespoons butter or
  margarine
1 teaspoon vanilla extract
2 medium bananas, sliced
Crumb-Nut Crust
Whipped topping
Chopped peanuts
Additional banana slices
Maraschino cherries

Crumb-Nut Crust
1¼ cups graham cracker crumbs
¼ cup finely chopped peanuts
⅓ cup butter or margarine,
  melted

▼ In medium saucepan, stir together sugar, cornstarch, cocoa and salt. Stir together milk and egg yolks; gradually stir into sugar mixture.

▼ Cook over medium heat, stirring constantly, until mixture thickens and comes to a boil. Reduce heat to low; boil, stirring constantly, 3 minutes. Remove from heat; stir in butter and vanilla. Press plastic wrap directly onto filling; cool about 20 minutes.

▼ Arrange banana slices over bottom of Crumb-Nut Crust. Pour filling over bananas; press plastic wrap onto filling. Refrigerate 3 to 4 hours. Remove plastic wrap; top pie with whipped topping.

▼ Garnish with chopped peanuts, banana slices and maraschino cherries. Refrigerate leftover pie. *8 servings.*

▼ CRUMB-NUT CRUST: Heat oven to 350°F. In medium bowl, stir together graham cracker crumbs, peanuts and butter. Press mixture on bottom and up sides of 9-inch pie plate. Bake 8 to 10 minutes or until lightly browned.

ℰASY MILK CHOCOLATE BAR PIE

¼ cup milk
16 marshmallows or 1½ cups
  miniature marshmallows
1 HERSHEY'S Milk Chocolate
  Bar (7 oz.), broken into pieces
1 cup (½ pt.) cold whipping
  cream
1 packaged crumb crust (6 oz.)

▼ In medium microwave-safe bowl, place milk and marshmallows. Microwave at HIGH (100%) 1 minute; stir well. If necessary, microwave at HIGH additional 15 seconds at a time, stirring after each heating, until marshmallows are melted.

▼ Add chocolate pieces; stir until chocolate is melted and mixture is smooth. Cool completely.

▼ In small mixer bowl, beat whipping cream until stiff; fold into chocolate mixture. Spoon into crust. Cover; refrigerate until firm, at least 4 hours. Cover refrigerate leftover pie. *6 to 8 servings.*

CREAMY CHOCOLATE TARTS

⅔ cup HERSHEY'S Semi-Sweet
   Chocolate Chips
¼ cup milk
1 tablespoon sugar
½ teaspoon vanilla extract
½ cup cold whipping cream
6 (4-oz. pkg.) single serve
   graham crusts
Sweetened whipped cream
Sliced fresh fruit, maraschino
   cherries or fresh mint

▼ In small microwave-safe bowl, place chocolate chips, milk and sugar. Microwave at HIGH (100%) 1 minute or until milk is hot and chips melt when stirred.

▼ Using whisk or rotary beater, beat until mixture is smooth; stir in vanilla. Cool to room temperature.

▼ In small mixer bowl, beat whipping cream until stiff; carefully fold chocolate mixture into whipped cream until blended. Spoon or pipe into crusts.

▼ Cover; refrigerate until set. Top with sweetened whipped cream. Garnish as desired.
6 servings.

TRIPLE DECKER CHOCOLATE COCONUT CREAM PIE

⅔ cup sugar
⅓ cup cornstarch
¼ teaspoon salt
3 cups milk
3 eggs, slightly beaten
1 tablespoon butter or margarine
2 teaspoons vanilla extract
½ cup flaked coconut
3 tablespoons HERSHEY'S
   Cocoa
3 tablespoons sugar
2 tablespoons milk
1 baked 9-inch pie crust, cooled
Whipped topping

▼ In medium saucepan, stir together ⅔ cup sugar, cornstarch, salt and 3 cups milk; blend in eggs. Cook over medium heat, stirring constantly, until mixture boils; boil and stir 1 minute.

▼ Remove from heat; stir in butter and vanilla. Into small bowl, pour 1½ cups cream filling; stir in coconut. Set aside.

▼ Stir together cocoa, 3 tablespoons sugar and 2 tablespoons milk; blend into remaining cream filling in saucepan. Return to heat; heat just to boiling, stirring constantly. Remove from heat; pour 1 cup chocolate filling into baked pie crust.

▼ Spread coconut filling over chocolate layer. Top with remaining chocolate filling; spread evenly. Cover with plastic wrap; refrigerate until cold. Just before serving, spread with whipped topping.
8 servings.

Creamy Chocolate Tarts

CHOCOLATETOWN PIE

½ cup (1 stick) butter or margarine, softened
2 eggs, beaten
2 teaspoons vanilla extract or 2 tablespoons bourbon
1 cup sugar
½ cup all-purpose flour
1 cup HERSHEY'S Semi-Sweet Chocolate Chips or HERSHEY'S MINI CHIPS Semi-Sweet Chocolate
1 cup chopped pecans or walnuts
1 unbaked 9-inch pie crust
Festive Whipped Cream (optional)

Festive Whipped Cream
½ cup cold whipping cream
2 tablespoons powdered sugar
¼ teaspoon vanilla extract or 1 teaspoon bourbon

▼ Heat oven to 350°F. In small mixer bowl, beat butter; add eggs and vanilla. Stir together sugar and flour; add to butter mixture. Stir in chocolate chips and nuts; pour into unbaked pie crust.

▼ Bake 45 to 50 minutes or until golden brown. Cool about 1 hour on wire rack; serve warm. Garnish with Festive Whipped Cream, if desired.
8 to 10 servings.

▼ FESTIVE WHIPPED CREAM: In small mixer bowl, combine whipping cream, powdered sugar and vanilla; beat until stiff.
About 1 cup topping.

Reese's Peanut Butter and Hershey's Kisses Layer Pie, Chocolatetown Pie

REESE'S PEANUT BUTTER & HERSHEY'S KISSES LAYER PIE

**18 HERSHEY'S KISSES Milk
  Chocolates**
**1 cup (½ pt.) whipping cream,
  divided**
1 baked 9-inch pie crust, cooled
**1 package (6-serving size) vanilla
  pudding and pie filling mix***
**½ cup REESE'S Creamy
  Peanut Butter**
2 cups milk
1 tablespoon powdered sugar
¼ teaspoon vanilla extract
**Additional HERSHEY'S KISSES
  Chocolates, (optional)**

▼ Remove wrappers from chocolate pieces. In small microwave-safe bowl, place chocolate pieces and 2 tablespoons whipping cream. Microwave at HIGH (100%) 1 minute or until chocolate is melted and mixture is smooth when stirred.

▼ Spread chocolate mixture over bottom of pie shell; refrigerate 30 minutes or until set.

▼ In 2-quart saucepan, place pudding mix and peanut butter. Using wire whisk, gradually blend in milk, stirring until smooth. Cook over medium heat, stirring constantly, until pudding thickens and boils; remove from heat.

▼ Cool 10 minutes; stirring frequently. Pour pudding over chocolate mixture in pie crust. Refrigerate several hours or until firm.

▼ In small mixer bowl, beat remaining whipping cream, powdered sugar and vanilla until stiff. Spread over top of pie. Garnish with additional chocolate pieces, if desired. Cover; refrigerate leftover pie.
8 servings.

*Do not use instant pudding mix.

INNKEEPER PIE

⅔ cup plus ¾ cup sugar, divided
⅓ cup HERSHEY'S Cocoa
1 cup water
⅓ cup butter or margarine
2½ teaspoons vanilla extract, divided
1 cup all-purpose flour
1 teaspoon baking powder
½ teaspoon salt
¼ cup shortening
½ cup milk
1 egg
Pastry Crust
½ cup chopped nuts
Sweetened Whipped Cream

Pastry Crust
1⅓ cups all-purpose flour
½ teaspoon salt
⅛ teaspoon baking powder
½ cup shortening
3 tablespoons cold water

Sweetened Whipped Cream
1 cup (½ pt.) cold whipping cream
2 tablespoons sugar
1 teaspoon vanilla extract

▼ Heat oven to 350°F. In medium saucepan, stir together ⅔ cup sugar and cocoa; stir in water. Cook over medium heat, stirring occasionally, until mixture boils; boil and stir 1 minute. Remove from heat; add butter and 1½ teaspoons vanilla, stirring until butter is melted. Set aside.

▼ In small mixer bowl, stir together flour, ¾ cup sugar, baking powder and salt; add shortening, milk and remaining 1 teaspoon vanilla. Beat on medium speed of electric mixer 2 minutes. Add egg; beat 2 minutes.

▼ Spoon batter into prepared Pastry Crust. Stir chocolate mixture; gently pour over batter. Sprinkle nuts over top.

▼ Bake 55 to 60 minutes or until wooden pick inserted in cake portion comes out clean. Cool slightly; serve warm with Sweetened Whipped Cream.
8 servings.

▼ PASTRY CRUST: In medium bowl, stir together flour, salt and baking powder. Cut in shortening until particles are size of small peas; sprinkle in water, tossing with fork until all flour is moistened. Roll dough into circle about ⅛ thick. Fit into 9-inch pie plate; flute edge.

▼ SWEETENED WHIPPED CREAM: In small mixer bowl, combine whipping cream, sugar, and vanilla; beat until stiff.

RICH CHOCOLATE CREAM PIE

1 package (6-serving size) vanilla
cook & serve pudding and pie
filling mix*
3 cups milk
2 cups (12-oz. pkg.) HERSHEY'S
Semi-Sweet Chocolate Chips or
1¾ cups(10-oz. pkg.)
HERSHEY'S Semi-Sweet
Chocolate Chunks
1 baked 9-inch pie crust, cooled
Whipped topping (optional)

▼ In medium saucepan,combine pudding and pie
filling and milk. Cook over medium heat, stirring
constantly, until mixture comes to full boil.

▼ Remove from heat; immediately add chocolate chips
to hot mixture, stirring until chips are melted and
mixture is smooth. Pour into baked pie crust.

▼ Place plastic wrap directly onto surface; refrigerate
several hours or overnight. Garnish with whipped
topping, if desired.
About 8 servings.

Do not use instant pudding mix.

Rich Chocolate Cream Pie, Innkeeper Pie

MIX AND MATCH BUTTERCREAM CENTERS

⅔ cup HERSHEY'S Semi-Sweet
  Chocolate Chips, REESE'S
  Peanut Butter Chips or
  HERSHEY'S Vanilla Milk
  Chips
½ cup (1 stick) butter, softened
¼ cup whipping cream
1 teaspoon vanilla extract
3½ to 4 cups powdered sugar,
  divided

▼ Cover tray with wax paper. In small microwave-safe bowl, place desired flavor of chips. Microwave at HIGH (100%) 30 seconds to 1 minute or until chips are melted when stirred.

▼ In small mixer bowl, beat butter, whipping cream and vanilla until fluffy; gradually blend in 1 cup powdered sugar. Gradually stir in melted chips and remaining 2½ to 3 cups powdered sugar, stirring until mixture holds its shape. If necessary, cover and refrigerate until mixture can be shaped.

▼ Shape mixture into 1-inch balls; place on prepared tray. Refrigerate until balls (centers) are firm and dry on surface, several hours or overnight. Coat with Simple Chocolate Coating, Peanut Butter Chip Coating or Vanilla Milk Chip Coating.
About 4 dozen centers.

PEANUT BUTTER CHIP COATING

1⅔ cups (10-oz. pkg.) REESE'S
  Peanut Butter Chips
2 tablespoons shortening (do not
  use butter, margarine or oil)

▼ Cover tray with wax paper. In top of double boiler, over hot, not boiling, water place chips and shortening; stir constantly until melted.

▼ With fork, one at a time, dip fruit, pretzels, cookies or desired Buttercream Centers into warm mixture. Quickly remove, shaking gently to remove excess coating; place on prepared tray.

▼ If candy centers are used, swirl small amount of melted mixture on top of coated candy for decoration. Let stand until set. Store loosely covered in cool, dry place.
About ¾ cup coating.

▼ **Variation**
VANILLA MILK CHIP COATING
Substitute 1⅔ cups (10-oz. pkg.) HERSHEY'S Vanilla Milk Chips for peanut butter chips. Follow dipping directions above.

SIMPLE CHOCOLATE COATING

2 cups (12-oz. pkg.) HERSHEY'S Semi-Sweet Chocolate Chips or HERSHEY'S MINI CHIPS Semi-Sweet Chocolate

2 tablespoons plus 2 teaspoons shortening (do not use butter, margarine or oil)

▼ Cover tray with wax paper. In medium heat-proof bowl, place chocolate chips and shortening. In separate large heat-proof bowl, put very warm water (100°to 110°F.) to 1-inch depth.

▼ Carefully place bowl with chocolate into bowl with water; water should come halfway up side of chocolate bowl. With dry rubber scraper, stir chocolate and shortening *constantly*, until chocolate and shortening are melted and mixture is smooth. Do *not* get water in bowl with chocolate. If water cools, replace it with very warm water as directed above.

▼ Remove chocolate bowl from inside water bowl. With fork, one at a time, dip chilled centers into chocolate mixture; gently tap fork on edge of bowl to remove excess chocolate.

▼ Invert coated center on prepared tray; swirl small amount of melted chocolate on top to cover fork marks. Let stand until firm. Store candies loosely covered in cool, dry place.
Coating for 3 to 4 dozen centers.

Mix and Match Buttercream Centers with Vanilla Milk Chip Coating, Peanut Butter Chip Coating, Simple Chocolate Coating

CHOCOLATE MINT SQUARES

6 tablespoons butter
½ cup HERSHEY'S Cocoa
2 cups powdered sugar
3 tablespoons plus 1 teaspoon milk, divided
1 teaspoon vanilla extract
Mint Filling

Mint Filling
1 package (3 oz.) cream cheese, softened
2 cups powdered sugar
½ teaspoon vanilla extract
¼ teaspoon peppermint extract
3 to 5 drops green food color

▼ Line 8-inch square pan with foil. In small saucepan over low heat, melt butter; add cocoa. Cook, stirring constantly, just until mixture is smooth.

▼ Remove from heat; add powdered sugar, 3 tablespoons milk and vanilla. Cook over low heat, stirring constantly, until mixture appears melted and glossy. Pour half of mixture into prepared pan; spread quickly. Refrigerate. Prepare Mint Filling; spread over chocolate layer. Refrigerate 10 minutes.

▼ To remaining chocolate mixture in saucepan, add remaining 1 teaspoon milk. Cook over low heat, stirring constantly, until chocolate is melted. Spread quickly over filling. Refrigerate until thoroughly chilled. Cut into squares. Store in refrigerator. *About 4 dozen candies.*

▼ MINT FILLING: In small mixer bowl, beat all ingredients until smooth. Add 2 to 3 teaspoons milk, if needed, for spreading consistency.

Chocolate Mint Squares

CHOCOLATE MARSHMALLOW SLICES

½ cup (1 stick) butter or
  margarine
2 cups (12-oz. pkg.)
  HERSHEY'S Semi-Sweet
  Chocolate Chips
6 cups (10½-oz. pkg.) miniature
  marshmallows
1 cup finely chopped nuts
Additional chopped nuts

▼ In medium saucepan over low heat, melt butter and chocolate chips, stirring constantly, until blended. Remove from heat; cool 5 minutes.

▼ Stir in marshmallows and 1 cup nuts; do not allow marshmallows to melt. On wax paper, shape mixture into two 7-inch rolls. Wrap in foil; refrigerate about 20 minutes.

▼ To coat rolls, roll in additional chopped nuts. Wrap; refrigerate overnight. Cut rolls into ¼-inch slices. Store in airtight container in cool, dry place.
About 3 dozen slices.

Chocolate Marshmallow Slices

CHOCOLATE TRUFFLES

¾ cup (1½ sticks) butter
¾ cup HERSHEY'S Cocoa
1 can (14 oz.) sweetened
   condensed milk
1 tablespoon vanilla extract
Cocoa or powdered sugar

▼ In heavy saucepan over low heat, melt butter. Add cocoa; stir until smooth. Blend in sweetened condensed milk; stir constantly until mixture is thick, smooth and glossy, about 4 minutes.

▼ Remove from heat; stir in vanilla. Refrigerate 3 to 4 hours or until firm.

▼ Shape into 1¼-inch balls; roll in cocoa or powdered sugar or a blend of these two ingredients. Refrigerate until firm, 1 to 2 hours. Store, covered, in refrigerator. *About 2½ dozen candies.*

▼ **Variations**
NUT TRUFFLES
Add ¾ cup coarsely chopped toasted pecans to chocolate mixture when adding vanilla. (To toast pecans: In ungreased shallow pan, spread ¾ cup pecan halves in single layer. Bake at 375°F, stirring occasionally, about 5 to 7 minutes. Cool before chopping.)

ESPRESSO TRUFFLES
Decrease vanilla to 1 teaspoon. Stir in 1¼ teaspoons powdered instant espresso or coffee with vanilla. Roll balls in cocoa or chopped nuts.

NUT-COATED TRUFFLES
Roll balls in chopped nuts.

1 Use a melon ball scoop or spoon to remove truffle mixture from bowl.

2 Roll spoonfuls of truffle mixture between hands to form balls. Keep hands and truffle mixture as cold as possible.

3 Roll truffles in assorted coatings and place in decorative candy cups for serving.

Chocolate Truffles

Foolproof Dark Chocolate Fudge

3 cups (1½ 12-oz. pkgs.)
  HERSHEY'S Semi-Sweet
  Chocolate Chips
1 can (14 oz.) sweetened
  condensed milk
Dash salt
1 cup chopped walnuts
1½ teaspoons vanilla extract

▼ Line 8-or 9-inch square pan with foil. In heavy saucepan over low heat, melt chips with sweetened condensed milk and salt.

▼ Remove from heat; stir in walnuts and vanilla. Spread evenly into prepared pan. Refrigerate 2 hours or until firm.

▼ Remove from pan; place on cutting board. Peel off foil; cut into squares. Store loosely covered at room temperature.
About 5 dozen pieces or 2 pounds.

Rich Cocoa Fudge

3 cups sugar
⅔ cup HERSHEY'S Cocoa or
  HERSHEY'S European Style
  Cocoa
⅛ teaspoon salt
1½ cups milk
¼ cup (½ stick) butter or
  margarine
1 teaspoon vanilla extract

▼ Line 8-or 9-inch square pan with foil; butter foil. In heavy 4-quart saucepan, stir together sugar, cocoa and salt; stir in milk.

▼ Cook over medium heat, stirring constantly, until mixture comes to full rolling boil. Boil, without stirring, to 234°F or until syrup, when dropped into very cold water, forms a soft ball which flattens when removed from water. (Bulb of candy thermometer should not rest on bottom of saucepan).

▼ Remove from heat. Add butter and vanilla. *Do not stir.* Cool at room temperature to 110°F (lukewarm).

▼ Beat with wooden spoon until fudge thickens and loses some of its gloss. Quickly spread into prepared pan; cool. Cut into squares.
About 36 pieces or 1¾ pounds.

▼ **Variation**
MARSHMALLOW-NUT COCOA FUDGE
Increase cocoa to ¾ cup. Cook fudge as directed. Add 1 cup marshmallow creme with butter and vanilla. *Do not stir.* Cool to 110°F (lukewarm). Beat 10 minutes; stir in 1 cup chopped nuts and pour into prepared pan. (Fudge does not set until poured into pan.)

CREAMY DOUBLE DECKER FUDGE

1 cup REESE'S Peanut Butter Chips
1 can (14 oz.) sweetened condensed milk, divided
1 teaspoon vanilla extract, divided
1 cup HERSHEY'S Semi-Sweet Chocolate Chips

▼ Line 8-inch square pan with foil: In small microwave-safe bowl, place peanut butter chips and ⅔ cup sweetened condensed milk. Microwave at HIGH (100%) 1 to 1½ minutes, stirring after 1 minute, until chips are melted and mixture is smooth when stirred.

▼ Stir in ½ teaspoon vanilla; spread evenly into prepared pan. In small microwave-safe bowl, place remaining sweetened condensed milk and chocolate chips; repeat above microwave procedure.

▼ Stir in remaining ½ teaspoon vanilla; spread evenly over peanut butter layer. Cover; refrigerate until firm. Cut into squares. Store tightly covered in refrigerator. *About 4 dozen pieces or 1½ pounds.*

Rich Cocoa Fudge, Creamy Double Decker Fudge, Foolproof Dark Chocolate Fudge

CRISPY COCOA BARS

¼ cup (½ stick) butter or
  margarine
¼ cup HERSHEY'S Cocoa
6 cups (10½-oz. pkg.) miniature
  marshmallows
5 cups crisp rice cereal

▼ Butter 13 x 9 x 2-inch pan. In large saucepan over low heat, melt butter; stir in cocoa and marshmallows.

▼ Cook over low heat, stirring constantly, until marshmallows are melted and mixture is smooth and well blended. Continue cooking and stirring 1 minute. Remove from heat.

▼ Add cereal; stir until well coated. Using buttered spatula or wax paper, press mixture evenly into prepared pan. Cool completely. Cut into bars. *About 24 bars.*

Chocolate Shoppe Dip with Apples, Strawberry Citrus Snack Blocks, Crispy Cocoa Bars

CHOCOLATE SHOPPE DIP WITH APPLES

Apple slices
HERSHEY'S Chocolate Shoppe
Topping (Butterscotch Caramel
Fudge or Chocolate Caramel
Fudge)

▼ Arrange apple slices on platter. (To keep apples from turning brown, dip in mixture of 1 cup water and 1 teaspoon lemon juice; drain.)

▼ To serve, dip apple slices into topping, warmed or at room temperature.

STRAWBERRY CITRUS SNACK BLOCKS

4 envelopes unflavored gelatin
½ cup cold water
2 cups orange juice, heated
   to boiling
1½ cups HERSHEY'S
   Strawberry Syrup

▼ In large heat-proof bowl, sprinkle gelatin over water; let stand 5 minutes. Add juice, stirring until gelatin is completely dissolved. Stir in syrup.

▼ Pour into 13 x 9 x 2-inch pan. Cover; refrigerate 4 hours or until firm. Cut into blocks with knife or into shapes with cookie cutters. Serve cold.
About 3 dozen blocks.

NO-BAKE COCOA HAYSTACKS

1½ cups sugar
½ cup (1 stick) butter or
   margarine
½ cup milk
½ cup HERSHEY'S Cocoa
1 teaspoon vanilla extract
3½ cups quick-cooking
   rolled oats
1 cup flaked coconut
½ cup chopped nuts

▼ In medium saucepan, combine sugar, butter, milk and cocoa. Cook over medium heat, stirring constantly, until mixture comes to full boil; remove from heat.

▼ Stir in remaining ingredients. Immediately drop by rounded teaspoonfuls onto wax paper. Cool completely. Store in cool, dry place.
About 4 dozen candies.

CHOCO-PEANUT BUTTER DROPS

2 cups (12-oz. pkg.) HERSHEY'S
   Semi-Sweet Chocolate Chips
1 can (14 oz.) sweetened
   condensed milk
1 cup miniature marshmallows
1 cup coarsely chopped peanuts
⅔ cup REESE'S Creamy
   Peanut Butter
2 teaspoons vanilla extract

▼ In medium saucepan, combine chocolate chips, sweetened condensed milk and marshmallows. Cook over low heat, stirring constantly, until marshmallows are melted and mixture is smooth.

▼ Remove from heat; stir in peanuts, peanut butter and vanilla. Spoon rounded teaspoonfuls into 1-inch paper candy cups or paper-lined small muffin cups.

▼ Cover; refrigerate at least 15 minutes before serving. Refrigerate leftover candies.
About 72 candies.

Note: Recipe may be halved.

CHEWY COCOA AND PEANUT BUTTER TREATS

1 cup light corn syrup
1 cup packed light brown sugar
1⅔ cups (10-oz. pkg.) REESE'S
   Peanut Butter Chips
¼ cup HERSHEY'S Cocoa
2 tablespoons butter or
   margarine
6 cups crisp rice cereal

▼ Butter 13 x 9 x 2-inch pan. In large saucepan, stir together corn syrup and brown sugar. Cook over medium heat, stirring constantly, until mixture comes to a boil.

▼ Remove from heat. Add peanut butter chips, cocoa and butter; stir until chips are melted and mixture is smooth. (Mixture will be thick.)

▼ Add cereal; stir until well coated. Immediately press into prepared pan. Cool thoroughly. Cut into squares.
About 30 treats.

CHOCOLATE NUT CLUSTERS

1 cup HERSHEY'S Milk
   Chocolate Chips
1 teaspoon shortening (do not
   use butter, margerine or oil)
1 cup broken pecans or walnuts

▼ In medium microwave-safe bowl, place chocolate chips and shortening. Microwave at HIGH (100%) 1 to 1½ minutes or until smooth when stirred. Stir in nuts.

▼ Spoon heaping teaspoonfuls into 1-inch paper candy cups or paper-lined small muffin cups, filling each cup about one-half full. Refrigerate until firm. Peel off paper cup, if desired.
14 to 16 candies.

Chocolate Nut Clusters, Choco-Peanut Butter Drops, Chewy Cocoa and Peanut Butter Treats

HERSHEY'S VANILLA MILK CHIPS ALMOND FUDGE

1⅔ cups (10-oz. pkg.) HERSHEY'S
Vanilla Milk Chips
⅔ cup sweetened condensed
milk
1½ cups coarsely chopped
slivered almonds, toasted*
½ teaspoon vanilla extract

▼ Butter 8-inch square pan. In medium saucepan over very low heat, melt vanilla milk chips and sweetened condensed milk, stirring constantly, until mixture is smooth.

▼ Remove from heat. Stir in almonds and vanilla. Spread in prepared pan. Cover; refrigerate until firm, about 2 hours. Cut into 1-inch squares.
About 4 dozen pieces or 1¾ pounds.

* To toast almonds: Spread almonds on cookie sheet. Bake at 350°F, stirring occasionally, 8 to 10 minutes or until lightly browned; cool.

PASTEL-COATED COCOA BONBONS

2 packages (3 oz. each) cream
cheese, softened
2 cups powdered sugar
½ cup HERSHEY'S Cocoa
2 tablespoons butter, melted
1 teaspoon vanilla extract
Pastel Coating

Pastel Coating
6 tablespoons butter
3 cups powdered sugar
¼ cup milk
1 teaspoon vanilla extract
Red, green or yellow food color

▼ In small mixer bowl, beat cream cheese. Add powdered sugar, cocoa, butter and vanilla; blend well. Cover; refrigerate several hours or until firm enough to handle.

▼ Place wax paper on tray. Shape mixture into 1-inch balls; place on prepared tray. Refrigerate, uncovered, 3 to 4 hours or until dry.

▼ Before coating, place in freezer about 10 minutes. Using fork, dip cold centers into very warm Pastel Coating. (Stir coating before dipping each bonbon.) Gently tap fork on side of bowl to remove excess coating. Quickly remove. Place on wax paper-covered tray.

▼ For decorative top, drizzle small amount coating over top of bonbon. Refrigerate until firm. Store in airtight container in refrigerator.
About 24 bonbons.

▼ PASTEL COATING: In medium microwave-safe bowl, combine butter, powdered sugar, milk and vanilla. Microwave at HIGH (100%) 1 to 2 minutes or until smooth when stirred. Add several drops desired food color to tint mixture pastel pink, green or yellow.

Hershey's Vanilla Milk Chips Almond Fudge, Pastel-Coated Cocoa Bonbons

CHOCOLATE DIPPED SNACKS

½ cup HERSHEY'S Milk
  Chocolate Chips
½ cup HERSHEY'S Semi-Sweet
  Chocolate Chips
1 tablespoon shortening (do not
  use butter, margarine or oil)
Potato chips, cookies, dried
  apricots or miniature pretzels

▼ Cover tray with wax paper. In small microwave-safe bowl, place chocolate chips and shortening. Microwave at HIGH (100%) 1 minute; stir. If necessary, microwave at HIGH additional 15 seconds at a time, stirring after each heating, just until chips are melted and mixture is smooth when stirred. Cool slightly.

▼ Dip ⅔ of each snack or fruit into chocolate mixture. Shake gently to remove excess chocolate. Place on prepared tray.

▼ Refrigerate, uncovered, about 30 minutes or until coating is firm. Store in airtight container in cool, dry place.
About ½ cup coating.

1 Dip snacks into melted chocolate mixture.

2 After dipping, shake gently to remove excess chocolate.

3 Place coated snacks on paper-covered tray and refrigerate.

CHOCOLATE MINT PATTIES

3⅔ cups (1 lb.) powdered sugar
¼ cup HERSHEY'S Cocoa
⅓ cup butter or margarine, softened
⅓ cup light corn syrup
1 teaspoon peppermint extract

▼ Sift together powdered sugar and cocoa; set aside. In large mixer bowl, beat butter, corn syrup and peppermint extract on medium speed of electric mixer until well blended.

▼ Gradually add 1 to 2 cups cocoa mixture, beating until well blended with wooden spoon, stir in remaining cocoa mixture. With hands, knead until mixture is well blended and smooth.

▼ On wax paper, pat or roll out to ¼-inch thickness. With small cookie cutters, cut into desired shapes *or,* using about 1 teaspoonful of chocolate mixture for each, shape into balls; flatten into patties. Garnish as desired. Store tightly covered in refrigerator. *About 7 dozen patties.*

Chocolate Dipped Snacks, Chocolate Mint Patties

CHOCO-ORANGE FLUFF

1 envelope unflavored gelatin
1/3 cup sugar
1/4 cup HERSHEY'S Cocoa
2 cups skim milk
1 teaspoon vanilla extract
1/8 to 1/4 teaspoon orange extract
1 1/2 cups frozen light non-dairy
whipped topping, thawed
Whipped topping (optional)
Fresh orange wedges (optional)

Nutritional information per serving
(1/8 recipe)
Calories 110, Protein 4 gm,
Carbohydrate 14 gm, Fat 4 gm,
Cholesterol 0 mg, Sodium 35 mg.

▼ In medium saucepan, stir together gelatin, sugar and cocoa. Stir in milk; let stand 2 minutes to soften. Cook over medium heat, stirring constantly, until gelatin is completely dissolved, about 5 minutes.

▼ Pour mixture into medium bowl; stir in vanilla and orange extracts. Refrigerate, stirring occasionally, until mixture mounds slightly when dropped from spoon (do not allow to gel).

▼ Add 1 1/2 cups whipped topping to chocolate mixture; beat with wire whisk until well blended. Refrigerate about 10 minutes to thicken slightly.

▼ Spoon into dessert dishes. Refrigerate 3 to 4 hours or until set. Garnish with whipped topping and orange wedges, if desired.
Eight 1/2 cup servings.

CHOCOLATE YOGURT CREME PUDDING

1 cup sugar
1/3 cup HERSHEY'S Cocoa
1 envelope unflavored gelatin
1 1/3 cups 2% lowfat milk
2 cups vanilla lowfat yogurt
1 teaspoon vanilla extract
Raspberries or sliced fresh
   strawberries

Nutritional information per serving
(1/8 recipe)
Calories 180, Protein 6 gm,
Carbohydrate 32 gm, Fat 2 gm,
Cholesterol 5mg, Sodium 25 mg.

▼ In medium saucepan, stir together sugar, cocoa and gelatin. Gradually stir in milk; let stand 5 minutes. Cook over medium heat, stirring constantly, until mixture comes to a boil and gelatin is dissolved. Cool slightly.

▼ Add yogurt and vanilla; blend gently just until well combined. Pour into dessert dishes. Refrigerate 6 hours or until set. Top with fruit.
8 servings.

Chocolate Yogurt Creme Pudding, Choco-Orange Fluff

LIGHTER COLD CHOCOLATE SOUFFLES

1 envelope unflavored gelatin
¼ cup cold water
2 tablespoons reduced-calorie tub margarine
1 cup skim milk
½ cup sugar
⅓ cup HERSHEY'S European Style Cocoa or HERSHEY'S Cocoa
½ cup cold skim milk
2½ teaspoons vanilla extract, divided
1 envelope (1.3 oz.) dry whipped topping mix

Nutritional Information per Serving
(⅙ recipe)
Calories 150, Protein 4 gm,
Carbohydrates 27 gm, Fat 3 gm,
Cholesterol 0 mg, Sodium 55 mg.

▼ Measure lengths of foil to fit around 6 small souffle dishes (4 oz. each); fold in thirds lengthwise. Lightly oil one side of foil; tape securely to outside of dishes (oiled side in) to form collar, allowing collar to extend 1 inch above rims of dishes.

▼ In small microwave-safe bowl, sprinkle gelatin over cold water; let stand 2 minutes. Microwave at HIGH (100%) 40 seconds; stir thoroughly.

▼ Stir in margarine until melted; let stand 2 minutes or until gelatin is completely dissolved. In small mixer bowl, blend 1 cup milk, sugar, cocoa and 2 teaspoons vanilla; gradually pour in gelatin mixture while beating on low speed of electric mixer.

▼ Prepare whipped topping mix as directed on package, using ½ cup cold milk and remaining ½ teaspoon vanilla; carefully fold into chocolate mixture until well blended.

▼ Spoon into prepared souffle dishes, allowing mixture to go ½-inch up collar. Cover; refrigerate until set, about 3 hours. Carefully remove foil. Serve cold. *6 servings.*

CHOCOLATE FRUIT DIP

1 container (8 oz.) vanilla yogurt
⅓ cup packed light brown sugar
1 tablespoon HERSHEY'S Cocoa
½ teaspoon vanilla extract
Dash ground cinnamon
Assorted fresh fruit

Nutritional Information per Serving
(2 tablespoons)
Calories 40, Protein 1 gm,
Carbohydrates 9 gm, Fat 0 gm,
Cholesterol 0 mg, Sodium 20 mg.

▼ In small bowl combine all ingredients except fruit. With whisk stir until smooth. Refrigerate until well chilled. Serve with fruit. Cover; refrigerate leftover dip. *About 1¼ cups dip.*

*L*IGHTER CHOCOLATE CREAM PIE

⅓ **cup sugar**

¼ **cup cornstarch**

3 **tablespoons HERSHEY'S European Style Cocoa or HERSHEY'S Cocoa**

2 **cups cold skim milk**

1 **teaspoon vanilla extract**

1 **packaged graham cracker crumb crust (6 oz.)**

Frozen non-dairy whipped topping, thawed (optional)

Fresh fruit (optional)

Nutritional Information per Serving
(¹⁄₁₀ recipe without garnish)
Calories 160, Protein 3 gm,
Carbohydrates 25 gm, Fat 5 gm,
Cholesterol 0 mg, Sodium 145 mg.

▼ In large microwave-safe bowl, stir together sugar, cornstarch and cocoa; gradually stir in milk. Microwave at HIGH (100%) 2 minutes; stir well.

▼ Microwave at HIGH 2 to 5 minutes or until mixture just begins to boil; stir well. Microwave at HIGH 30 seconds to 1 minute until mixture is very hot and thickened. Pour into crust.

▼ Place plastic wrap directly onto surface; refrigerate several hours or until firm. Garnish with whipped topping and fresh fruit, if desired.
10 servings.

Lighter Chocolate Cream Pie, Chocolate Fruit Dip, Lighter Cold Chocolate Souffles

CHOCOBERRY REFRESHER

1 container (8 oz.) vanilla
  lowfat yogurt
1¼ cups cold lowfat 2% milk
¼ cup HERSHEY'S Syrup
¼ cup HERSHEY'S Strawberry
  Syrup
Ice cubes (optional)

Nutritional Information per Serving
(8 oz.)
Calories 170, Protein 8 gm,
Carbohydrates 30 gm, Fat 3 gm,
Cholesterol 12 mg, Sodium 118 mg.

▼ In blender container, place yogurt, milk, chocolate
syrup and strawberry syrup. Cover; blend until
smooth. Serve over ice, if desired.
About three 8-ounce servings.

SECRET STRAWBERRY FILLED ANGEL CAKE

1 package (about 15 oz.) angel
  food cake mix
1 envelope unflavored gelatin
¼ cup cold water
1 cup (8 oz.) vanilla lowfat
  yogurt
⅓ cup HERSHEY'S Strawberry
  Syrup

▼ Mix, bake and cool cake as directed on package.
In small microwave-safe bowl, sprinkle gelatin
over cold water; let stand 2 minutes. Microwave at
HIGH (100%) 40 seconds; stir thoroughly. Let
stand 2 minutes or until gelatin is completely
dissolved; cool slightly.

▼ In medium bowl, stir together yogurt, strawberry
syrup and gelatin mixture until smooth; refrigerate
until mixture mounds slightly when dropped
from spoon.
(continued)

1 Prepare cake filling by slicing
layer from top of cake.

2 Carefully remove the inside of
the cake to form "trench."

3 Spoon the filling into the
"trench" and replace the cake top.

Chocolate Syrup Whipped Cream

Chocolate Syrup Whipped Cream
1 cup (½ pt.) cold whipping cream
¼ HERSHEY'S Syrup
⅛ teaspoon cream of tartar

Nutritional Information per Serving
(¹⁄₁₈ recipe)
Calories 120, Protein 3 gm,
Carbohydrates 19 gm, Fat 4 gm,
Cholesterol 15 mg, Sodium 80 mg.

▼ Place cake rounded side down. Using serrated knife, cut 1-inch layer from top of cake; lift off in one piece. Set aside.

▼ Using serrated knife, cut trench in cake 1 inch wide and 1 ½ inches deep, leaving 1-inch-wide inner and outer walls of cake. Using fork, carefully remove cake in trench without breaking through sides or bottom.

▼ Spoon strawberry syrup mixture into trench. Cover with reserved cake top. Cover; refrigerate while preparing Chocolate Syrup Whipped Cream. Spread evenly over top and sides of cake.

▼ Cover; refrigerate 4 hours or until center is set. Serve cold. Refrigerate leftover cake.
18 servings.

▼ CHOCOLATE SYRUP WHIPPED CREAM: In small mixer bowl, combine whipping cream, chocolate syrup and cream of tartar until stiff.

Chocoberry Refresher, Secret Strawberry Filled Angel Cake

Chocolate Sauce and Ice Milk, Chocolate Banana Lowfat Cupcakes

CHOCOLATE BANANA LOWFAT CUPCAKES

2 cups all-purpose flour
¾ cup sugar, divided
¼ cup HERSHEY'S Cocoa or
   HERSHEY'S European Style
   Cocoa
¾ teaspoon baking soda
½ teaspoon baking powder
¼ teaspoon salt
1 container (8 oz.) plain lowfat
   yogurt (1.5% milkfat)
½ cup mashed ripe banana
¼ cup skim milk
⅓ cup canola oil
2 teaspoons vanilla extract
3 egg whites
White Glaze

White Glaze
½ cup powdered sugar
3 to 4 teaspoons warm water

Nutritional information per serving
(1 cupcake)
Calories 130, Protein 2 gm,
Carbohydrate 22 gm, Fat 4 gm,
Cholesterol 0 mg, Sodium 110 mg.

▼ Heat oven to 350°F. Line muffin pans with foil paper bake cups (2 ½ inches in diameter). In large bowl, stir together flour, ¼ cup sugar, cocoa, baking soda, baking powder and salt; set aside.

▼ In medium bowl, stir together yogurt, banana, milk, oil and vanilla; set aside.

▼ In small mixer bowl, beat egg whites until soft peaks form. Gradually add remaining ½ cup sugar, beating until stiff peaks form.

▼ Stir yogurt mixture into flour mixture until moistened; fold in one-third of egg white mixture. Gently fold in remaining egg white mixture. Fill muffin cups ¾ full with batter.

▼ Bake 20 to 25 minutes or until wooden pick inserted in center comes out clean. Cool completely. Drizzle with White Glaze.
20 cupcakes.

▼ WHITE GLAZE: In small bowl, stir together powdered sugar with water; beat until smooth and of desired consistency.

CHOCOLATE SAUCE AND ICE MILK

2 tablespoons margarine
⅓ cup sugar
2 tablespoons HERSHEY'S
   Cocoa
2 tablespoons light corn syrup
1/4 cup evaporated skim milk
1 teaspoon vanilla extract
Vanilla ice milk

Nutritional information per serving
(1 tablespoon sauce with ½ cup ice milk)
Calories 150, Protein 3 gm,
Carbohydrate 24 gm, Fat 5 gm,
Cholesterol 10 mg, Sodium 85 mg.

▼ In small saucepan over low heat, melt margarine. Remove from heat; stir in sugar, cocoa and corn syrup. Stir in evaporated skim milk.

▼ Cook over low heat, stirring constantly, just until mixture begins to boil and is smooth.

▼ Remove from heat; stir in vanilla. Cool slightly. Spoon 1 tablespoon warm sauce over ½ cup vanilla ice milk for each serving.
¾ cup sauce, about 12 servings.

CHOCOLATE CHERRY ANGEL DELIGHT

⅓ cup HERSHEY'S Cocoa
1 package (about 15 oz.) "two-step" angel food cake mix
1 envelope (1.3 oz.) whipped topping mix
½ cup cold skim milk
½ teaspoon vanilla extract
1 can (20 oz.) reduced-calorie cherry pie filling

Nutritional information per serving
(¹⁄₁₄ recipe)
Calories 170, Protein 4 gm,
Carbohydrate 39 gm, Fat 0 gm,
Cholesterol 0 mg, Sodium 135 mg.

▼ Move oven rack to lowest position. In small bowl, sift cocoa over contents of cake flour packet; stir to blend. Proceed with mixing cake as directed on package.

▼ Bake and cool as directed for 10-inch tube pan. Using serrated knife, cut cake horizontally to make three layers.

▼ Prepare topping mix as directed on package, using skim milk. Fold one-half of pie filling into whipped topping. Place one cake layer on serving plate; spread with one-half of whipped topping mixture. Repeat procedure, ending with plain layer on top. Spoon remaining pie filling over top. Refrigerate leftover dessert.
14 servings.

Chocolate Cherry Angel Delight

CHOCO-LIGHT MUFFINS

1 ½ cups all-purpose flour
¾ cup granulated sugar
¼ cup HERSHEY'S Cocoa or
   HERSHEY'S European Style
   Cocoa
2 teaspoons baking powder
1 teaspoon baking soda
½ teaspoon salt
⅔ cup vanilla lowfat yogurt
⅔ cup skim milk
½ teaspoon vanilla extract
Powdered sugar (optional)

Nutritional information per serving
(¹⁄₁₄ recipe)
Calories 100, Protein 2 gm,
Carbohydrate 22 gm, Fat <1 gm,
Cholesterol 0 mg, Sodium 200 mg.

▼ Heat oven to 400°F. Paper-line muffin cups
(2 ½ inches in diameter). In medium bowl, stir
together flour, granulated sugar, cocoa, baking powder, baking soda and salt; stir in yogurt, milk and
vanilla just until combined. Do not beat. Fill each
muffin cup ⅔ full with batter.

▼ Bake 15 to 20 minutes or just until wooden pick
inserted in center comes out clean. Cool slightly in
pan on wire rack. Sprinkle with powdered sugar, if
desired. Serve warm.
14 muffins.

Choco-Light Muffins

Sunburst Chocolate Cake

3 eggs or 5 egg whites
¾ cup sugar
½ cup all-purpose flour
⅓ cup HERSHEY'S Cocoa
½ teaspoon baking soda
¼ teaspoon salt
⅓ cup water
1 teaspoon vanilla extract
Citrus Filling

Citrus Filling
1 envelope (1.3 oz.) whipped
   topping mix
½ cup cold skim milk
1 can (11 oz.) mandarin orange
   segments, drained and divided
¾ teaspoon grated orange peel

Nutritional information per serving
(⅟₁₂ recipe)
Calories 120, Protein 3 gm,
Carbohydrate 23 gm, Fat 2 gm,
Cholesterol 55 mg, Sodium 100 mg.

▼ Heat oven to 375°F. Grease sides and bottom of two 8-inch round baking pans; line bottoms with wax paper. In small mixer bowl, beat eggs on high speed of electric mixer 3 minutes. Gradually add sugar; continue beating 2 minutes. Remove from mixer.

▼ Stir together flour, cocoa, baking soda and salt; add alternately with water and vanilla to sugar mixture, folding gently until mixture is combined. Spread batter evenly into prepared pans.

▼ Bake 15 to 17 minutes. Cool 5 minutes; remove from pans and peel off paper. Cool completely.

▼ Place one cake layer on serving plate; spoon one-half Citrus Filling onto layer. Top with remaining layer and filling; garnish with reserved mandarin oranges. Cover; refrigerate several hours.
12 servings.

▼ CITRUS FILLING: In small bowl, beat topping mix with milk until stiff peaks form. Reserve ½ cup orange segments for garnish. Cut remaining segments into thirds; fold with orange peel into topping.

Chocolate Dessert Timbales

1 envelope unflavored gelatin
½ cup cold water
⅓ cup sugar
3 tablespoons HERSHEY'S Cocoa
1½ cups milk
2 egg yolks, slightly beaten
2 teaspoons vanilla extract
1 cup frozen non-dairy whipped
   topping, thawed
Additional whipped topping
Fresh or canned fruit slices,
   drained

Nutritional information per serving
(⅙ recipe)
Calories 150, Protein 5 gm,
Carbohydrate 18 gm, Fat 6 gm,
Cholesterol 75 mg, Sodium 40 mg.

▼ In small bowl, sprinkle gelatin over cold water; let stand several minutes to soften. In medium saucepan, combine sugar and cocoa; gradually stir in milk. Stir in egg yolks. Cook over medium heat, stirring constantly, until mixture just begins to boil; remove from heat.

▼ Add gelatin mixture and vanilla; stir until gelatin is completely dissolved. Transfer to medium bowl; refrigerate, stirring occasionally, until mixture begins to set, about 1 hour.

▼ Carefully fold 1 cup whipped topping into chocolate mixture, blending until smooth. Pour into 6 small custard cups; refrigerate until set. Garnish with whipped topping and fruit slices.
6 servings.

CHOCOLATE-BANANA SHERBERT

**1 cup mashed ripe banana
(about 2 bananas)**
**1 cup apricot nectar, peach or
pineapple juice, divided**
**½ cup HERSHEY'S Semi-Sweet
Chocolate Chips**
2 tablespoons sugar
1 cup milk

Nutritional information per serving
(⅛ recipe)
Calories 130, Protein 2 gm,
Carbohydrate 22 gm, Fat 4 gm,
Cholesterol 5 mg, Sodium 15 mg.

▼ Into blender container or food processor, slice bananas. Add ¾ cup fruit juice; blend until smooth.

▼ In small microwave-safe bowl, place chocolate chips, remaining ¼ cup fruit juice and sugar. Microwave at HIGH (100%) 30 seconds; stir. Add to mixture in blender; blend until thoroughly combined. Add milk; blend until smooth.

▼ Pour into 9-inch square pan or two ice cube trays. Cover; place in freezer until hard around edges, about 2 hours.

▼ Into large mixer bowl or food processor, spoon partially frozen mixture; beat or process until smooth but not melted. Cover; freeze until firm, stirring several times before mixture freezes. Scoop into dessert dishes. Serve frozen.
8 servings.

Chocolate Dessert Timbales

CHOCOLATE PUDDING PARFAITS

²/₃ **cup sugar**
¼ **cup HERSHEY'S Cocoa**
3 tablespoon cornstarch
Dash salt
2 ½ cups cold skim milk, divided
1 tablespoon light corn oil spread
1¼ teaspoons vanilla extract,
  divided
1 envelope (1.3 oz.) whipped
  topping mix
¼ **teaspoon freshly grated orange**
  peel
Orange slices (optional)

Nutritional information per serving
(¹/₇ recipe)
Calories 160, Protein 4 gm,
Carbohydrate 32 gm, Fat 2 gm,
Cholesterol 0 mg, Sodium 95 mg.

▼ In medium saucepan, combine sugar, cocoa, corn-starch and salt; gradually stir in 2 cups milk. Cook over medium heat, stirring constantly, until mixture boils; boil and stir 1 minute.

▼ Remove from heat; blend in corn oil spread and 1 teaspoon vanilla. Pour into medium bowl. Press plastic wrap onto surface of pudding; refrigerate until slightly cool.

▼ In small mixer bowl, combine topping mix, remaining ½ cup milk and ¼ teaspoon vanilla; prepare according to package directions. Fold ½ cup whipped topping into pudding.

▼ Blend orange peel into remaining topping. Alternately spoon or pipe chocolate pudding and orange flavored whipped topping into parfait glasses. Refrigerate until cold. Garnish with orange slices, if desired. *7 servings.*

▼ Variation
LITE CHOCOLATE MINT PARFAITS
Omit orange peel. Increase vanilla to 1½ teaspoons and add ¼ teaspoon mint extract and 3 to 4 drops red food color.

1 For an easier and cleaner fill, place mixtures into pastry bags. Pipe chocolate mixture into bottom of glass.

2 Alternate layers of mixtures.

3 Finished parfaits ready for serving.

Peachy Chocolate Cake

1 ½ cups all-purpose flour
1 cup sugar
¼ cup HERSHEY'S Cocoa
1 teaspoon baking soda
½ teaspoon salt
1 cup water
¼ cup vegetable oil
1 tablespoon white vinegar
1 teaspoon vanilla extract
2 cups canned peaches

Nutritional information per serving
(¹⁄₁₂ recipe)
Calories 180, Protein 2 gm,
Carbohydrate 31 gm, Fat 5 gm,
Cholesterol 0 mg, Sodium 160 mg.

▼ Heat oven to 350°F. Grease and flour two 8-inch round baking pans. In a large mixing bowl, stir together flour, sugar, cocoa, baking soda and salt.

▼ Add water, oil, vinegar and vanilla; stir until smooth and thoroughly blended. Pour into prepared pans.

▼ Bake 20 to 25 minutes or until wooden pick inserted in center comes out clean. Cool 10 minutes; remove from pans to wire racks. Cool completely.

▼ Just before serving place one layer on serving plate; arrange one-half of peaches on layer. Top with second layer and remaining peaches.
12 servings.

Peachy Chocolate Cake, Chocolate Pudding Parfaits

QUICK CHOCOLATE CUPCAKES

1½ cups all-purpose flour
¾ cup sugar
¼ cup HERSHEY'S Cocoa
1 teaspoon baking soda
½ teaspoon salt
1 cup water
¼ cup vegetable oil
1 tablespoon white vinegar
1 teaspoon vanilla extract

Nutritional information per serving
(1 cupcake without frosting)
Calories 95, Protein 1 gm,
Carbohydrate 16 gm, Fat 3 gm,
Cholesterol 0 mg, Sodium 105 mg.

▼ Heat oven to 375°F. Paper-line muffin cups (2½ inches in diameter). In medium bowl, stir together flour, sugar, cocoa, baking soda and salt. Add water, oil, vinegar and vanilla; beat with wire whisk just until batter is smooth and ingredients are well blended.

▼ Pour batter into paper bake cups, filling each ⅔ full. Bake 16 to 18 minutes or until wooden pick inserted in center comes out clean. Cool; frost as desired. *18 cupcakes.*

CHOCOLATE CAKE FINGERS

1 cup sugar
1 cup all-purpose flour
⅓ cup HERSHEY'S Cocoa
¾ teaspoon baking powder
¾ teaspoon baking soda
½ cup skim milk
¼ cup frozen egg substitute, thawed
¼ cup canola oil
1 teaspoon vanilla extract
½ cup boiling water
Powdered sugar
1 teaspoon freshly grated orange peel
1½ cups frozen light non-dairy whipped topping, thawed
30 fresh strawberries or raspberries (optional)

Nutritional information per serving
(2 pieces)
Calories 110, Protein 1 gm,
Carbohydrate 15 gm, Fat 5 gm,
Cholesterol 0 mg, Sodium 50 mg.

▼ Heat oven to 350°F. Line bottom of 13 x 9 x 2-inch baking pan with wax paper. In large mixer bowl, stir together sugar, flour, cocoa, baking powder and baking soda.

▼ Add milk, egg substitute, oil and vanilla; beat on medium speed of electric mixer 2 minutes. Add water, stirring with spoon until well blended. Pour batter into prepared pan.

▼ Bake 16 to 18 minutes or until wooden pick inserted in center comes out clean. With knife or metal spatula, loosen cake from edges of pan.

▼ Place towel on wire rack; sprinkle with powdered sugar. Invert cake on towel; peel off wax paper. Turn cake right side up. Cool completely.

▼ Cut cake into small rectangles (about 2 x 1¼ inches). Stir orange peel into whipped topping; spoon dollop on each piece of cake. Garnish with strawberry or raspberry, if desired. *42 pieces.*

Quick Chocolate Cupcakes, Chocolate Cake Fingers

HERSHEY'S LIGHT CHOCOLATE CAKE

1¼ cups all-purpose flour
⅓ cup HERSHEY'S Cocoa
1 teaspoon baking soda
6 tablespoons extra light corn oil spread
1 cup sugar
1 cup skim milk
1 tablespoon white vinegar
½ teaspoon vanilla extract
Light Cocoa Frosting

Light Cocoa Frosting
1 envelope (1.3 oz.) dry whipped topping mix
½ cup cold skim milk
1 tablespoon HERSHEY'S Cocoa
½ teaspoon vanilla extract

Nutritional information per serving
(¹⁄₁₂ recipe)
Calories 160, Protein 3 gm,
Carbohydrate 28 gm, Fat 4 gm,
Cholesterol 0 mg, Sodium 115 mg.

▼ Heat oven to 350 F. Spray two 8-inch round baking pans with cooking spray. In bowl, stir flour, cocoa and baking soda; set aside. In saucepan, melt corn oil spread; stir in sugar. Remove from heat.

▼ Add milk, vinegar and vanilla to mixture in saucepan; stir. Add dry ingredients; whisk until well blended. Pour evenly into pans.

▼ Bake 20 minutes or until wooden pick inserted in center comes out clean. Cool. Place 1 layer on serving plate; spread Light Cocoa Frosting over top. Place second layer on top; frost top of cake. Refrigerate. *12 servings.*

▼ LIGHT COCOA FROSTING: In small mixer bowl, stir together whipped topping mix, milk, cocoa and vanilla. Beat on high speed of mixer about 4 minutes or until soft peaks form.

Hershey's Light Chocolate Cake, Hershey's Ricotta Cheesecake,

CHOCOLATE RICOTTA CHEESECAKE

Yogurt Cheese
⅓ cup graham cracker crumbs
3½ cups (two 15-oz. containers)
lowfat part-skim ricotta cheese,
drained)
2 egg whites
¾ cup sugar
⅓ cup HERSHEY'S Cocoa
2 tablespoons all-purpose flour
2 teaspoons vanilla extract
Sliced fresh strawberries and
kiwifruit

Yogurt Cheese
2 containers (8 oz. each) vanilla
lowfat yogurt, no gelatin added

Nutritional information per serving
(¹⁄₁₆ recipe)
Calories 150, Protein 9 gm,
Carbohydrate 18 gm, Fat 5 gm,
Cholesterol 20 mg, Sodium 110 mg.

▼ Prepare Yogurt Cheese. Heat oven to 325°F. Sprinkle crumbs on bottom of 9-inch springform pan.

▼ In food processor bowl or large mixer bowl, process ricotta cheese until smooth. Add Yogurt Cheese, egg whites, sugar, cocoa, flour and vanilla; process just until well blended. Pour over crumbs.

▼ Bake 50 minutes or until edges are set. Turn off oven; open oven door slightly. Leave cheesecake in oven 1 hour. Remove from oven.

▼ With knife, loosen cake from side of pan. Cool completely; remove side of pan. Refrigerate before serving. Garnish with fruit. Cover; refrigerate leftover cheesecake.
16 servings.

▼ YOGURT CHEESE: Line a non-rusting colander or sieve with large piece of double thickness cheesecloth; place colander over deep bowl. Spoon yogurt into prepared colander; cover. Refrigerate until liquid no longer drains from yogurt, about 24 hours. Remove yogurt from cheesecloth; discard liquid.

SILKY COCOA CREME

1 envelope unflavored gelatin
¼ cup cold water
½ cup sugar
⅓ cup HERSHEY'S Cocoa
¾ cup skim milk
½ cup lowfat part-skim
ricotta cheese
1 teaspoon vanilla extract
½ cup frozen light non-dairy
whipped topping, thawed
Fresh strawberries

Nutritional information per serving
(⅛ recipe)
Calories 110, Protein 4 gm,
Carbohydrate 17 gm, Fat 3 gm,
Cholesterol 5 mg, Sodium 35 mg.

▼ In small bowl, sprinkle gelatin over water; allow to stand 2 minutes to soften. In medium saucepan, stir together sugar and cocoa; stir in milk.

▼ Cook over medium heat, stirring constantly, until mixture is very hot. Add gelatin mixture, stirring until gelatin is dissolved; pour into medium bowl. Refrigerate until mixture is slightly cold (do not allow to gel).

▼ In blender or food processor bowl, beat ricotta cheese and vanilla until smooth; stir into whipped topping. Gradually fold into cocoa mixture; pour into 2-cup mold. Refrigerate until set. Unmold; serve with strawberries.
8 servings.

New York Chocolate Egg Cream

¼ cup Cocoa Syrup
¼ cup light cream
½ cup club soda, freshly opened

Cocoa Syrup
1½ cups sugar
¾ cup HERSHEY'S Cocoa
Dash salt
1 cup hot water
2 teaspoons vanilla extract

▼ Cocoa Syrup, light cream and club soda should be cold. In tall glass, place ¼ cup Cocoa Syrup; stir in light cream to blend. Slowly pour soda down side of glass, stirring constantly. Serve immediately.
One 8-ounce serving.

▼ COCOA SYRUP: In medium saucepan, stir together sugar, cocoa and salt. Gradually add water, stirring to keep mixture smooth. Cook over medium heat, stirring constantly, until mixture boils; boil and stir 3 minutes. Remove from heat; stir in vanilla. Cool. Cover; refrigerate. Use as topping for ice cream and desserts or for chocolate-flavored drinks.
About 2 cups syrup.

Cappuccino Cooler

1½ cups cold coffee
1½ cups chocolate ice cream
¼ cup HERSHEY'S Syrup
Whipped cream

▼ In blender container, place all ingredients except whipped cream. Cover; blend until smooth. Serve immediately over crushed ice. Garnish with whipped cream.
About four 6-ounce servings.

▼ **Variation**
Substitute vanilla ice cream for chocolate; increase syrup to ⅓ cup.

Chocolate Root Beer Float

1 tablespoon sugar
2 teaspoons HERSHEY'S Cocoa
1 tablespoon hot water
1 scoop vanilla ice cream
Cold root beer

▼ In 12-oz. glass, stir together sugar and cocoa; stir in water. Add ice cream; fill glass with root beer. Stir; serve immediately.
One 12-ounce serving.

New York Chocolate Egg Cream, Cappuccino Cooler

$\mathcal{H}$OT COCOA

½ cup sugar
¼ HERSHEY'S Cocoa
Dash salt
⅓ cup hot water
4 cups (1 qt.) hot milk
¾ teaspoon vanilla extract
Miniature marshmallows or
  sweetened whipped cream
  (optional)

▼ In medium saucepan, stir together sugar, cocoa and salt; blend in water. Cook over medium heat, stirring constantly, until mixture comes to a boil. Boil and stir 2 minutes.

▼ Add milk; stirring constantly, heat to serving temperature. *Do not boil.* Remove from heat; add vanilla.

▼ Beat with rotary beater or whisk until foamy. Serve topped with miniature marshmallows or whipped cream, if desired.
Five 8 ounce servings.

▼ **Variations**
SPICED COCOA
Add ⅛ teaspoon ground cinnamon and ⅛ teaspoon ground nutmeg with vanilla extract. Serve with cinnamon stick, if desired.

MINT COCOA
Add ½ teaspoon mint extract or 3 tablespoons crushed hard peppermint candy or 2 to 3 tablespoons white creme de menthe with the vanilla extract. Serve with a peppermint candy stick, if desired.

CITRUS COCOA
Add ½ teaspoon orange extract or 2 to 3 tablespoons orange liqueur.

SWISS MOCHA
Add 2 to 2½ teaspoons powdered instant coffee with vanilla extract.

COCOA AU LAIT
Omit whipped cream. Spoon 2 tablespoons softened vanilla ice cream on top of each cup cocoa at serving time.

SLIM-TRIM COCOA
Omit sugar. Combine cocoa, salt and water; substitute skim milk. Proceed as above. With vanilla, stir in sugar substitute with sweetening equivalence of ½ cup sugar.
(continued)

CANADIAN COCOA
Add ½ teaspoon maple extract with vanilla extract.

MICROWAVE SINGLE SERVING
In microwave-safe cup or mug, combine 1 heaping teaspoon HERSHEY'S Cocoa, 2 heaping teaspoons sugar and dash salt. Add 2 teaspoons cold milk; stir until smooth. Fill cup with milk. Microwave at HIGH (100%) 1 to 1½ minutes or until hot. Stir to blend; serve.

Hot Cocoa

Chocolate Soda, Chocolate Shake

CHOCOLATE SODA

¼ cup cold club soda,
  freshly opened
3 tablespoons HERSHEY'S
  Syrup
2 scoops vanilla ice cream
Additional cold club soda

▼ In tall glass, stir together ¼ cup soda and syrup; add ice cream. Fill glass with additional soda; stir lightly. Serve immediately.
One 12-ounce serving.

▼ **Variation**
DOUBLE CHOCOLATE SODA
Substitute chocolate ice cream for vanilla ice cream.

CHOCOLATE SHAKE

2 cups cold milk
2 cups (1 pt.) vanilla ice cream,
  divided
¾ cup HERSHEY'S Syrup

▼ In blender container, place milk, 1 cup ice cream and syrup. Cover; blend until smooth. Pour into glasses; top with scoops of remaining ice cream.
About three 10-ounce servings.

▼ **Variations**
Before blending, add one of the following: 1 ripe, medium banana, sliced, or ⅔ cup drained, canned peach slices, or ½ teaspoon mint extract, or ½ cup crushed, sweetened strawberries.

FROSTY CHERRY FLOAT
Add 3 tablespoons maraschino cherry juice before blending.

FROSTY PEANUT FLOAT
Add 1 tablespoon REESE'S Creamy Peanut Butter before blending.

CHOCOLATE CITRUS COOLER

1½ cups cold milk
¼ cup frozen orange juice
  concentrate, thawed
3 tablespoons HERSHEY'S
  Syrup
1 scoop vanilla ice cream
Crushed ice or additional
  ice cream (optional)

▼ In blender container, place milk, orange juice concentrate, syrup and 1 scoop ice cream. Cover; blend until smooth. Pour into glasses over ice or top with additional ice cream, if desired.

About three 8-ounce servings.

Chocolate Citrus Cooler

STRAWBERRY ICE CREAM SODA

¼ **cup cold club soda,**
  freshly opened
2 to 3 tablespoons HERSHEY'S
  Strawberry Syrup
3 small scoops vanilla ice cream
Additional club soda

▼ In tall glass, stir together ¼ cup club soda and syrup. Add ice cream; fill glass with additional club soda. Stir gently; serve immediately.
1 serving.

▼ **Variation**
  CHOCOLATE ICE CREAM SODA
  Substitute 3 tablespoons HERSHEY'S Syrup for strawberry syrup; prepare as directed above.

Strawberry Ice Cream Soda

Frozen Banana Smoothie

1 cup cold milk or half-and-half
½ cup mashed ripe banana
   (about 1 medium)
½ cup creme de banana
   (banana-flavored liqueur)
⅓ cup HERSHEY'S Syrup
2½ cups ice cubes

▼ In blender container, place all ingredients. Cover; blend on high speed 2 minutes. Reduce speed; blend 1 minute longer or until frothy. Serve immediately. *About three 9-ounce servings.*

Chocolate Mint Smoothie

1 cup milk, divided
2 tablespoons HERSHEY'S
   Cocoa
2 tablespoons sugar
⅛ teaspoon mint extract
1 cup vanilla ice cream
Mint leaves (optional)

▼ In blender container, place ½ cup milk, cocoa and sugar. Cover; blend well. Add remaining ½ cup milk, mint extract and ice cream. Cover; blend until smooth. Serve immediately. Garnish with mint leaves, if desired. *About two 8-ounce servings.*

Orange Chocolate Float

½ cup orange juice
2 tablespoons HERSHEY'S
   Syrup
1 tablespoon sugar
Crushed ice
Whipped cream
Orange slice (optional)

▼ In blender container, place orange juice, syrup and sugar. Cover; blend. Pour over ice in glass; top with whipped cream. Garnish with orange slice, if desired. Serve immediately. *One 6-ounce serving.*

Frozen Banana Smoothie, Chocolate Mint Smoothie

CHOCOLATE CUT-OUTS

1 Spread melted chocolate on wax paper covered tray. Refrigerate.

2 Use knife or cookie cutters to cut through chocoolate layer. Refrigerate.

3 Carefully peel wax paper away from chocolate. Cover and refrigerate until ready to use.

1 cup HERSHEY'S Semi-Sweet Chocolate Chips

▼ In microwave-safe bowl, place chocolate chips. Microwave at HIGH (100%) 1 minute; stir. On wax paper-covered cookie sheet, spread melted chocolate with spatula. Chill 5 to 8 minutes or just until chocolate begins to set.

▼ With sharp knife or cookie cutters, score chocolate into triangles, hearts or other shapes. *Do not* try to separate at this time. Cover; chill several hours or until very firm.

▼ Carefully peel wax paper away from chocolate; gently separate shapes at score marks. Place on tray; cover and refrigerate until ready to use.

CHOCOLATE CURLS

HERSHEY'S Milk Chocolate Bar, SPECIAL DARK BAR, or Unsweetened Baking Chocolate

▼ The secret to successful curls is chocolate at the proper temperature, slightly warm but still firm. On a warm day, room temperature might be fine.

▼ Place unwrapped chocolate on cookie sheet. Place incooled oven until warm. (Or Microwave on HIGH (100%) about 30 seconds or just until chocolate feels slightly warm.)

▼ With even pressure draw vegetable peeler along underside of chocolate; a curl will form. Refrigerate until firm.

▼ Use side of candy bar for narrow curls. Use width of one or two blocks for medium-size curls. Use entire width of bar for large curls.

1 With even pressure, draw vegetable peeler along underside of slightly warm chocolate bar. A curl will form naturally

2 Chocolate curls are very delicate. Use wooden pick to lift curl to wax-paper covered tray.

3 Finished curls ready for garnishing desserts.

CHOCOLATE ROSETTES

¼ **cup sugar**
2 **tablespoons HERSHEY'S**
   Cocoa
½ **cup cold whipping cream**
½ **teaspoon vanilla extract**

▼ In small mixer bowl, stir together sugar and cocoa. Stir in whipping cream and vanilla. Beat until stiff. Fit decorating bag with large rosette tip; spoon chocolate cream into bag. Pipe rosettes on top of ice cream cake.

1 Hold bag at angle slightly above surface of cake. Squeeze bag and move hand in circular motion back to starting point.

2 Stop squeezing and pull tip away.

GRATED CHOCOLATE

▼ To grate chocolate for garnishing, select a firm bar of semi-sweet or milk chocolate. Grated chocolate may be sprinkled over a surface or arranged in a design.

1 Rub chocolate piece over grater, letting chocolate shreds fall onto a piece of wax paper.

2 Chocolate may be grated to create a variety of sizes.

3 Grated chocolate should be stored in refrigerator.

Peanut Butter Cups

1⅔ cups (10-oz.pkg.) REESE'S
   Peanut Butter Chips
1 tablespoon plus 2 teaspoons
   shortening (do not use butter,
   margarine or oil)

▼ Paper-line 12 muffin cups (2½ inches in diameter). In microwave-safe bowl, place peanut butter chips and shortening. Microwave at HIGH (100%) 1½ minutes or until smooth when stirred.

▼ With narrow pastry brush, thickly and evenly coat inside pleated surface and bottom of each paper cup with peanut butter mixture.

▼ Refrigerate coated cups 10 minutes; recoat any thin spots. (If necessary, microwave peanut butter mixture 30 seconds to thin.) Tightly cover cups; refrigerate until firm.

▼ Remove only a few peanut butter shells from refrigerator at a time; carefully peel paper from each cup. (Will keep weeks in an airtight container in refrigerator.)

▼ Variation
CHOCOLATE CUPS
Substitute 2 cups (12-oz. pkg.) HERSHEY'S Semi-Sweet Chocolate Chips for REESE'S Peanut Butter Chips. Follow directions above.

1 Brush melted peanut butter chip mixture into paper cups.

2 Carefully remove paper cups from each chilled peanut butter chips cup.

3 Peanut butter and chocolate cups ready for filling.

CHOCOLATE SILHOUETTES

1 Trace a drawing on paper and place under a sheet of wax paper. Both sheets of paper should be on a firm surface such as a cookie sheet or tray.

2 Spoon melted chocolate into a pastry bag fitted with a writing tip. Following the drawing under the wax paper, pipe chocolate in a steady flow to outline the drawing.

3 Crisscross the design from side to side to fill the center.

2 cups (12-oz. pkg.) HERSHEY'S Semi-Sweet Chocolate Chips

▼ Draw desired size heart shapes on paper; cover with wax or parchment paper. Place both sheets of paper on baking sheet or tray. In microwave-safe bowl., place chocolate chips. Microwave at HIGH (100%) 1 to 1½ minutes or until chips are melted when stirred.

▼ Place chocolate in small pastry bag fitted with writing tip on wax paper, following heart outlines, pipe chocolate into heart shaps. Fill in center of hearts with a crisscross of chocolate to connect the sides.

▼ Refrigerate until hearts are firm. Carefully peel wax-paper away from chocolate hearts. Place on tray. Refrigerate until ready to use.

CHOCOLATE LEAVES

1 Brush melted chocolate on underside of non-toxic leaf. Avoid getting chocolate on front of leaf.

2 Carefully peel leaves away from chocolate.

3 Place leaves on tray and refrigerate until ready to use.

Several ivy, lemon, rose or other non-toxic leaves
½ cup HERSHEY'S Semi-Sweet Chocolate Chips
1 teaspoon vegetable shortening

▼ Thoroughly wash and dry leaves. In small microwave-safe bowl, place chocolate chips and shortening. Microwave at HIGH (100%) 45 seconds to 1 minute or until chips are melted when stirred.

▼ With small soft-bristled brush, brush melted chocolate onto backs of leaves being careful not to drip over edges; place on wax-paper covered tray or rack.

▼ Refrigerate until very firm. Carefully peel fresh leaves from chocolate leaves; refrigerate until ready to use.

▼ **Variation**
VANILLA LEAVES
Substitute ½ cup HERSHEY'S Vanilla Milk Chips for chocolate chips.

ſAUCE PAINTING

1   Place raspberry sauce in plate and drops of cream on sauce.

2   Use wooden pick to pull cream from one dot to another.

3   Finished plate ready for dessert to be added.

▼ Sauce painting is an attractive way to serve cake, cheesecake or any dessert which will be served on a plate. Select a plain dessert or dinner plate without a design. The two sauces should have the same consistency for even distribution.

▼ Start by spooning the background sauce onto plate to evenly coat plate. Do not get sauce on rim. Drop contrasting sauce in desired design. A variety of sauces may be used including fruit purees, thin pudding mixes, HERSHEY'S Syrup, HERSHEY'S Strawberry Syrup, pie glazes and melted jelly.

1   Place chocolate sauce on plate Spiral cream on sauce.

2   Use wooden pick to pull from center through rings to outside of plate. Then pull from outside of plate toward center.

3   Finished plate ready for dessert to be added.

BORDERS AND FRILLS

1 A large open star tip may be used for a broad fluted border, stars, individual shells or a shell border.

2 A writing tip may be used for printing, writing or outlining.

▼ Make cakes, cookies and other desserts more personal by using some of these extra touches. Borders and frills may be made with frosting or whipped cream. Frostings should be stiffer than the frosting used to frost the sides and top of the cake. Whipped cream should be stiffly beaten and used just before serving.

▼ Purchase reusable decorating bags, disposable bags or parchments bags to decorate your desserts. A few basic decorating tips shown here are all that are needed to get you started on creating your own special desserts.

3 A small star tip may be used for a narrow fluted border, stars or rosettes.

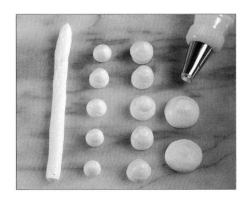

4 A smooth round tip may be used for a broad smooth border or balls of various sizes.

ℋELPFUL HERSHEY HINTS

🐾 HERSHEY'S baking chocolate products will stay fresh for well over a year if stored in a cool, dry place with a constant temperature of 60°F to 70°F. Do not refrigerate; keep well wrapped.

🐾 Bloom, the gray film that sometimes appears on chocolate chips and bars, occurs when chocolate is exposed to varying temperatures or has been stored in damp conditions. Bloom does not affect the taste or quality of the chocolate.

🐾 Chocolate can be melted in a double boiler or a microwave oven. Because chocolate scorches easily, using direct heat is not recommended. To melt in double boiler, place HERSHEY'S chocolate chips or baking bars in top of double boiler over hot, not boiling, water; stir constantly until melted. Remove from over heat.

To melt in microwave, place HERSHEY'S chocolate chips or baking bars in a microwave-safe bowl. Microwave for minimum time specified in recipe and then immediately stir. (Chocolate will not change appearance or appear melted.) If more melting time is required, microwave at 15 second intervals and stir until melted.

🐾 A wet utensil or condensation of steam droplets can cause chocolate to get stiff and grainy. If this happens stir in 1 teaspoon solid vegetable shortening (not butter or margarine) for every 2 ounces chocolate.

🐾 HERSHEY'S Cocoa keeps very well when stored at room temperature in the original container. It retains its freshness and quality almost indefinitely if sealed securely. Do not refrigerate.

🐾 HERSHEY'S Cocoa may be used in place of unsweetened baking chocolate in most recipes. 3 tablespoons HERSHEY'S Cocoa plus 1 tablespoon shortening or oil equals 1 bar (1 oz.) unsweetened baking chocolate.

🐾 Butter and margarine are interchangeable if both are listed in the ingredient list. Do not use lowfat spreads, soft or tub margarine unless recipe specifically calls for these ingredients. They act differently in baking and cooking and may cause unsatisfactory results.

HELPFUL HERSHEY HINTS

☙ Assemble all ingredients needed in a recipe before you start. For best baking results, ingredients, except eggs, should be at room temperature. Eggs should be removed from the refrigerator no more than 30 minutes before using them. Use fresh ingredients in baking, especially baking powder, baking soda and spice.

☙ To soften butter for a recipe let stand at room temperature for 30 to 45 minutes. To soften in the microwave, for ½ cup (1 stick) leave in parchment wrapper or remove foil wrapper and place on wax paper or microwave-safe plate. Microwave at DEFROST (30% power) for 30 to 40 seconds, turning every 10 seconds.

☙ Neufchatel cheese is a lower fat alternative for cream cheese. You will find it in the dairy case near the cream cheese. It may be used as a substitute for cream cheese but will result in slightly different taste and texture.

☙ If using oven-proof glass bakeware, reduce oven temperature by 25 degrees to prevent overbaking. Baking a cake in too large a pan will result in a flat, shrunken cake. Too small a pan might cause batter to overflow and cake will bulge and lose its shape.

☙ Shiny pans are preferred for baking cakes and cookies since they reflect heat and will produce light, delicate crusts. Use dull metal or glass pie plates to produce crisp, brown crusts.

☙ Store soft cookies in container with tight fitting lid. Store crisp cookies in container with loose fitting lid. Store bar cookies in the pan in which they were baked; cover pan with foil or plastic wrap.

☙ Refrigerate pies with custard or cream fillings as soon as they have cooled. Cakes with whipped cream, cream cheese or cream fillings, frostings or toppings also should be refrigerated. After serving, cover leftover pie or cake and refrigerate immediately.

☙ For best results when baking, make a single recipe. Never double or triple candy recipes because candy requires specific evaporation and cooking rates which are affected by quantities.